The Guide to High Definition Video Production

Preparing for a Widescreen World

REBO Studio in association with Clay Gordon

Focal Press
Boston Oxford Melbourne Singapore Toronto Munich New Delhi Tokyo

Focal Press is an imprint of Butterworth-Heinemann.

A member of the Reed Elsevier group

Recognizing the importance of preserving what has been written, Butterworth–Heinemann prints its books on acid-free paper whenever possible.

Library of Congress Cataloging-in-Publication Data

The guide to high definition video production : preparing for a widescreen world / REBO Studio in association with Clay Gordon.
p. cm.
Includes index.
ISBN 0-240-80265-9 (pbk.)
1. Video recordings—Production and direction. 2. High definition television.
I. Gordon, Clay, 1958- . II. REBO Studio.
PN1992.94.G85 1996
791.45'0232—dc20 95-50845
CIP

British Library Cataloguing-in-Publication Data
A catalogue record for this book is available from the British Library.

The publisher offers special discounts on bulk orders of this book.
For information, please contact:
Manager of Special Sales
Butterworth–Heinemann
313 Washington Street
Newton, MA 02158–1626
Tel: 617-928-2500
Fax: 617-933-2620

For information on all Focal Press publications available, contact our World Wide Web home page at: http://www.bh.com/bh/

10 9 8 7 6 5 4 3 2 1

Printed in the United States of America

Table of Contents

List of Figures

List of Tables

Acknowledgments

I could neither have begun nor completed this book without the input, support, hard work, dedication, and vision of Barry Rebo, Tomio Taki, Kathy Scott, Barry Minnerly, Randy Bradley, Abby Levine, Steven Dupler, Neil Smith, Alan Miller, Mark Forker, David Steinberg, and the dozens of other patient colleagues and friends I have met through REBO Studio over the past five years.

I would also like to thank John Alonzo; Randall P. Dark and Charles Pantuso of HD VISION, Inc.; C.R. Caillouet of Caillouet Technical Services; Philip Hack of NHK Enterprises, America; Noriko T. Mukai of Tokyo Broadcasting System; Janet West and Milan Krsljanin of Sony Broadcast and Professional, Europe; Lou Levinson of the MCA/MEI HD Telecine Research Center; Barry Clark of Telenova; Siegfried Steiner of Steiner Film (Munich); Keith Melton of Infinity Filmworks; Graham Andrews and Tim Volker of Creative Technology Ltd. (London); Rick Smolan of Against All Odds Productions; Jay Schmalholz; Jimmy O'Donnell; and Clinton Cowels. Your interest, contributions, support, and patience are very highly valued and appreciated.

To all of them, as well as to all of you who are embarking on your own High Definition video productions, this book is dedicated.

Clay Gordon

December, 1995

Production Notes

Text for this book was prepared using an ancient version of Acta from Symmetry Software, and the most recent version of Nisus Writer from Nisus Software, Inc.

Program stills included in this book were digitized from UNIHI videotape using a REBO Research ReStore™ , a High Definition videographics device attached to a Macintosh computer. Transparencies were scanned using Kodak's PhotoCD process. FPO thumbnails for layout purposes were scanned using an HP ScanJet IICX flatbed scanner. Where neccssary, digitized images were manipulated in Adobe Photoshop.

Line illustrations were created using Adobe Illustrator.

The book was produced using Adobe FrameMaker. The body text is set in Adobe Garamond. Headings and captions are set in Univers Condensed.

With the exception of digitizing and processing the images that appear herein and the final layout of the book, all production was done on my trusty Apple Macintosh PowerBook 160 computer that celebrated its third birthday in the midst of final production. And which, despite its advanced age (for a computer), hardly complained at all.

FaxPro from Delrina, EudoraPro from Qualcomm, and a Zoom ZFX model 410 28.8 external faxmodem were used to connect my computer to the rest of the world.

Peace of mind through regular backups and mass file transfers were made possible by an Iomega ZIP 100MB removable cartridge drive; Symantec's Norton Utilities for Macintosh and Symantec Anti-Virus for Macintosh also made it easier for me to sleep at night.

Picture Credits

Production still photography courtesy of Abby Levine, Clay Gordon, and REBO Studio. Individual copyrights are held by the photographers.

Trademark Notices

ReStore™ , ReScan™ , ReLay™ , and ReFlect™ are trademarks of REBO Research/REBO Group, L.P. All other registered and trademarked names, words, and phrases belong to their registered owners.

Chapter 1

Introduction

A look back over the past century shows how the introduction of a new imaging tool has invariably changed not only the physical means of production but the creative content as well.

Advances in computer, digital video, and digital audio technologies have dramatically changed—and will continue to change—the ways we educate ourselves, the ways we entertain ourselves, the ways we do business, the ways new ideas are brought to reality: the ways we communicate.

High Definition video imaging tools are bringing about powerful and fundamental changes in both the perception and execution of visual storytelling. We are once again using new tools to create new visions and new perspectives.

Computers coupled with High Definition video imaging capabilities are destined to become a dominant imaging medium of the late 1990s and beyond—a medium in which higher resolution, wider screen digital imagery will be used as the foundation for all forms of education, entertainment, business, design, and communication.

Preface

The Guide to High Definition Video Production, Preparing for a Widescreen World is not about the politics of selecting a High Definition Television or an all-digital Advanced Television transmission system. It's also not your average technical production and engineering handbook. We won't pretend that if you study this book closely you'll know *everything* you need to know about the basics of conventional film or video production. We assume that you already went to film school or have a job in film or video, that you know something about production, or that you sleep with a dog-eared copy of the American Society of Cinematographers' *American Cinematographer Manual* on the bedside table. Or maybe you're just curious about this thing called HDTV. This book is not rocket science, either, so you won't need an advanced degree in theoretical physics, quantum mechanics, or electrical engineering to get through it. You can leave your pocket calculator turned off and your slide rule in its case. Sure, the material does get technical at times, but we've tried very hard to make it all understandable and to make the technical parts of the book interesting—maybe even fun at times—to read.

So, if that's what this book is *not* about, what *is* it about?

It's about pioneering. It's about the experiences of a small—and growing—dedicated group of very talented and very creative people who have spent much of the last decade pursuing a wider vision. This book is for people who are interested in joining that group of pioneers and expanding the scope of their own vision.

It's about High Definition *video* and not just High Definition *Television*. Throughout this book, we are careful to draw a distinction between High Definition *video*, a term which we use to refer to all formats of high resolution, widescreen video, and High Definition *Television* (as defined in the Society of Motion Picture and Television Engineers (SMPTE) 240M/260M specification) which is a specific format of High Definition video. In the same vein, the term standard definition video is used to mean 4:3 aspect ratio NTSC, PAL, and SECAM video.

Most importantly, though, this is a practical book. This is a book for people who are in the business of producing film or video and who want to know more about what High Definition video production is *really* like—from single-camera, film-style documentary production all the way to multicamera live music to sporting events.

It's for people who are tired of reading articles about what HDTV or Advanced Television (ATV) might be, or will be, or should be, or could be, five or ten years from now. This book is for people who want to know the nuts and bolts and ins and outs of what it takes to produce High Definition video programming today.

This book is a distillation of the knowledge and expertise of some of the most experienced High Definition video producers, engineers, directors, and DPs in the world. They tell you what they have learned—usually the hard way—about what works and what doesn't; lessons that have been learned on hundreds of High Definition video productions stretching back into the earliest days of commercial HDTV production—still less than a decade ago.

We've tried to present the real issues that face producers when contemplating a High Definition video production. The unvarnished truth, tips, tricks, things to keep in mind, situations to avoid, the inside skinny that the manuals never tell you, all mixed in with some interesting and, we hope, amusing stories.

When you get done reading this book you should have a better understanding of the real differences between producing and engineering film, traditional video, and High Definition video.

To facilitate this process, the book is organized into sections that follow the production process from preproduction all the way through to postproduction. There's a section that covers the basics of High Definition video technology for people who want to become more familiar with that, a glossary section to help you understand technical terms, and a section devoted to help you understand some of the creative considerations that differentiate High Definition video production from traditional video and film production.

It is certainly our hope that when you get done reading this book you'll have a better appreciation of what it takes to produce High Definition video and that you'll be inspired to go out and produce High Definition video programming of your own. Those who do will find themselves in the midst of a world that will be undergoing dramatic changes in the next few years as High Definition production, transmission, and projection technology mature. It promises to be a wild ride and one that will be a lot of fun.

REBO and High Definition: The Early Years

I had my first introduction to HDTV in 1986 at the NAB convention in Dallas. I remember looking at the various demonstrations on monitors and projectors and not being terrifically impressed—especially when I heard how much everything cost.

I was reacquainted with HDTV in 1990 when I visited REBO Studio for the first time, investigating the use of high-speed, high-resolution imaging technologies for a publishing client who wanted to digitize a large quantity of images quickly. Conventional flatbed and transparency scanning was too slow, and the files created were too large to work with conveniently. Video capture, while fast enough, was not of sufficiently high resolution. We wondered if HDTV could work for us. It was certainly fast enough, and the resolution was a good compromise between video and print.

This time when I looked at the images on the HDTV monitor, I realized that I was looking at a technology that could do what I wanted. I can still recall the feeling that I had looking at the pictures—that HDTV was something special. I also knew then that HDTV production was something I wanted to get involved in, and within six months, I was working at REBO investigating ways of using HDTV for nonbroadcast and nontelevision applications.

When Barry Rebo first looked at HDTV in the very early 1980s, he also was not impressed with the demonstrations he saw. They weren't interesting to him, because they showed that the equipment was dramatically ill-equipped to go out into the field, the very place where he had pioneered film-style portable NTSC video production almost a decade earlier.

> "I think that there were three groups of imagemakers in the early 1970s," Barry said, recalling how he first got involved in video production. "The first group consisted of the people who worked with film and were used to working with a single camera and relying on heavy editing and postproduction. They came from the tradition of the classic cinema, creating works for theatrical release and for television.
>
> "The second group consisted of the people working in live television and live-to-tape. They were primarily event oriented, working in news, sporting events, variety shows, and concerts, but also doing situation comedies and relying on television oriented postproduction.
>
> "The third group consisted of people who were coming to video as a new experience. These were the people who came to video in the early days but who thought like filmmakers; shooting on location, using a single camera, and making use of film-style postproduction. This is the group I felt I belonged to.
>
> "The first realistic portable video production tools we had to work with were the black-and-white portapaks, which quickly evolved into inexpensive color cameras with helical-scan recorders. But the real breakthrough was the time base corrector (TBC) which made it possible to stabilize the footage we shot with these inexpensive portable packages and make it suitable for transmission.
>
> "With the TBC, this new generation of video equipment finally became interesting to broadcasters, essentially making possible the whole era of electronic news gathering and electronic field production. By the mid 1970s, when the equipment was finally proven in the field as viable, the stage was set for the development of the hard news programs and the video magazine format.

"When I saw the first tests of HDTV in the early 1980s, the fact that the equipment couldn't go out into the field told me that although it could make pretty pictures, it wasn't production-ready yet.

"It was during the 1984 Olympics in Los Angeles that I began to understand where High Definition video was going. Those Olympics saw the introduction of the Super-Slo-Mo system, which was based on the basic research performed on HDTV. The difference was that instead of processing and displaying 30 frames of high-resolution video every second, Super-Slo- Mo processed and displayed 90 frames of 525-resolution video every second. In other words, Super-Slo-Mo used the increased processing power and bandwidth to increase resolution in the time domain rather than to increase the pictures' size or quality."

It was while trying to explain the concept of Super-Slo-Mo to his partner, Tomio Taki, that Barry became more interested in the original application of the High Definition video research, which was high-resolution, conventional frame-rate video for making movies.

"It wasn't until the Fall SMPTE conference in 1985 that I knew that High Definition video was for real. One of the demonstrations that year was a comparison, in HDTV and 35mm, of a short film produced by the Italian broadcaster RAI. The films were being projected side by side with a curtain in between them. I remember ducking my head back and forth between the two screens as I had this epiphany: 'This is what I really wanted to do, to make the transition between television and theatrical films.' And I knew then that I could use High Definition video to make the transition.

"A couple of months later I was in Europe scouting a project with Neil Smith, another partner in REBO at the time, and we visited David Niles in Paris when he still was the only one doing actual production in High Definition video there. By the time we got back to the States, I was more convinced than ever that High Definition video was what I wanted to do next."

In March 1986, REBO placed its first order for HDTV production equipment. The order consisted of a Sony HDC–100 (tube) camera, 4 Sony HDV–1000 (analog) VTRs, assorted high definition monitors, a Sony analog switcher, and a specially modified Ultimatte for video compositing. Added up, the order totalled over $1.5 million.

It turned out to be no mean feat for REBO to actually buy the equipment. Nobody would finance the purchase or write a lease, because nobody knew what HDTV was or how REBO would be able to cover the lease.

"I remember that I needed to get the order and a deposit check to Sony in a hurry, because I was on my way back to Europe for a shoot," Barry recalls. "I remember driving out to Sony's headquarters in Montvale, New Jersey in the driving rain, nervous that I wouldn't make it before they closed. I got there and they were waiting for me. I don't think they really believed I was going to show up.

"When I handed over the order and the check, they popped a bottle of champagne and handed me a tape box that had been signed by everybody there—a memento of the first ever sale of High Definition video production and postproduction equipment in the United States."

It ended up taking Sony a long time to deliver the entire equipment order. It was not until September or October.

"In retrospect," Barry admits, "it turned out to be a big break for us. By the time all of the gear arrived, I realized that what we had to do was to find an outrageous director to work on that first project. By then I had also come to realize the significance of the blue screen capabilities afforded by High Definition video.

"I've often wished that I had a tape recording of the first time I called Zbigniew Rybczinski. His English at the time was poor, but he agreed to come and meet with me to discuss my ideas. When we met I found out that he was a chain-smoking madman but obviously a genius. He clearly grasped the implications of what I was talking about."

Zbig had the rights to do a film of John Lennon's *Imagine*, but no money to do it with. REBO ended up finding funding for a music video for the song *Candy* by the group Cameo and decided to just shoot *Imagine* immediately afterward using whatever money was left over from the Cameo shoot.

Figure 1.1—Still from Candy

Once the projects were set, it was up to Barry Minnerly and Abby Levine, two very talented engineers who had been with REBO studio for many years by that time, Neil Smith, the DP, and Alan Miller, the editor, to figure out how to make Zbig's ideas work. And they were pretty radical ideas—shooting and editing live in the camera.

"The Sony equipment arrived from Japan without manuals in English, the Ultimatte arrived from California (with manuals in English) and," Barry said, "inside a week or so, we were on location shooting *Candy* and *Imagine*. We went from 0 to 150 m.p.h. right out of the starting blocks.

"I think what really hooked us frankly, was making *Imagine* with Zbig and going through the process of learning how to make this magical realism using the new High Definition video gear. We were forced, in a very short period of time, to learn about a whole new medium."

Figure 1.2—Still from Imagine

Somewhere along the way, REBO decided to push what they were doing all the way out past the edge, and take *Imagine* all the way through to transferring it to 35mm film and entering it into competition in the 1987 Cannes Film Festival in the Short Film Live Action category. What in October was only an ill-formed concept—not just ideas for videos, but the whole question of how to produce in this new medium—in spring was in competition in Cannes.

Imagine did not win at Cannes that year, but it achieved the distinction of being the first short film accepted into competition at Cannes that was produced entirely in High Definition video.

In 1989 another REBO-produced High Definition video short film, *Performances Pieces*, starring F. Murray Abraham, did win at Cannes.

Figure 1.3—Still from Performance Pieces

Imagine was a prodigious technical effort, and its acceptance into the competition probably reflected that fact. It was really just a music video without any dialog, but it got there.

"Once we achieved the success at Cannes," Barry continued, "we were convinced that working in the new medium was a no-brainer. We couldn't believe that no one else was following us... that what we were doing was truly a rarity.

"There was an excitement and an innocence about using this new equipment. What I was proudest of were the people I was working with at the time and the way we reached out into the independent artist community when there were no efforts by the Hollywood film establishment to do so.

"In a way, it mirrored the reasons I started REBO Production Associates in 1975. I couldn't find anyone who shared my vision of the way to use portable video gear and who would hire me. I ended up having to go out and do it for myself and hiring people who shared my vision. That's the way it was in 1986 with High Definition video as well."

A Brief History of HDTV

Development work on what is now called HDTV began in Japan in the late 1960s. The first commercial introduction of HDTV production equipment in the United States began in 1986, although some prototype production and postproduction equipment was in use in the United States as early as 1984.

The first HDTV broadcast occurred in 1989. Produced by NHK and transmitted live from Lincoln Center in New York City to Tokyo, the broadcast of *Our Common Future* marked the inauguration of an experimental one hour per day MUSE broadcast service.

Regularly scheduled commercial satellite HDTV broadcasting in Japan began on 1125 day—November 25, 1991—also using the MUSE system. The compression technology originally used in MUSE could not squeeze an HDTV channel into a standard NTSC 6 MHz channel; 8 MHz was required by MUSE to achieve acceptable picture quality. A variation of MUSE called Narrow MUSE is capable of compressing an HDTV signal down to 6 MHz.

Milestones in High Definition Video Production

Year	Date	Event
1986	March	REBO writes check for first HDTV production equipment in North America.
	September	Equipment arrives.
	October, November	In production on music videos: *Candy* and *Imagine.*
1987	Q1	RAI: *Julia and Julia* is the first feature shot in HDTV (Italy).
	March, April	In production on *White Hot,* REBO's first feature film project.
	May	*Imagine* goes to Cannes.
	June	REBO participates in the first International Electronic Cinema Festival in Montreux.
	Q3	SMPTE 240M specification published. Aspect ratio changes from 5:3 to 16:9.

1987	Q4	CBC: *Chasing Rainbows* is the first miniseries shot in HDTV in North America.
1988	January	REBO starts producing commercials for Sony, Reebok, Kentucky Fried Chicken, and others.
	Q2	Advanced Television Test Center (ATTC) formed.
	June	REBO wins Astrolabium for *Sharaku* at the International Electronic Cinema Festival.
	Q3	NHK: *Olympic Games* shot in HDTV. Bell System ships HDTV over fiber optics.
	Q1	CBS: *The Littlest Victims* TV movie for NTSC release shot in HDTV.
1989	April	NAB: REBO Research debuts the ReStore™, a low cost graphics device for postproduction; the ReScan™, an inexpensive downconverter, and ReLay™, a single fiber broadcast-quality analog fiber optic transmission system.
	Q2	NHK: MUSE DBS begins. REBO in production on *Performance Pieces.* ATTC and Cable Labs agree to cooperate in tests.
	Q3	*Performance Pieces* wins at Cannes. REBO in production on *Infinite Escher.*
1990	Q2	NHK/Comsat: closed circuit HDTV convert via HD-BMAC. ATTC tests first proponent. GI: first digital ATV proponent.
	May	REBO trades up to the Sony HDC–300 camera, and the HDD–1000 digital VTR; Now working in 16:9.
	Juno	REBO wins Astrolabium for *Televolution* at the International Electronic Cinema Festival.
	Q3	REBO in production on *Manhattan Music Magazine*; live, multicamera music series.
1991	Q2	NHK: Underwater HDTV documentary.
	June	REBO wins Astrolabium for *The Pigeon Man* at the International Electronic Cinema Festival.
	Q3	REBO in production on *Fool's Fire.*
	Q4	NHK/IRS: *Sting* Live NTSC PPV concert from Telesat HDTV mobile truck
	November 25	1125 day in Japan.
1991	Q4	FCC Report: Broadcasters get channels.
1992	Q1	NHK: *Winter Olympic Games* in HDTV
	Q2	REBO moves its postproduction to the left coast; HDLA opens in Burbank. FCC Update: NTSC to be phased out by 2008.
	Q3	NHK: *Summer Olympic Games* in HDTV. REBO goes to IAAPA with HDTV preshow for Iwerks' *Sub Oceanic Shuttle.*
	Q4	NHK/RVI: *Dylan* Live NTSC PPV concert from 240M/NTSC hybrid system. ATTC completes first round of tests.
	November, December	REBO in production on *The Astronomer's Dream*, their first project with the Sony HDC–500 camera.
1993	Q1	NHK: *NBA All-Star Game.*
	Q2	TBS: *Masters* Golf. FCC gets new chair and members. ATTC begins second round of tests.
	May	Grand Alliance formed.
	Q4	Introduction of portable Panasonic production package. REBO shoots *Clearwater* documentary on the Hudson River. ATTC completes second test round. FCC decision on standard delayed.
1994	March	REBO in production on *Passage to Vietnam.*
	June	REBO wins Chiba City Mayor's Award for *The White House: Inside with the President's Photographers* at the International Electronic Cinema Festival.
	Q3	*World Cup Soccer* broadcast live and in HD around the world.
	November	REBO in production on *Doctor's Without Borders* in France, Russia, and Africa.
1995	June	REBO wins Astrolabium for *New York: On the Edge, "Gender Outlaws"* at the International Electronic Cinema Festival.
	December 6	FCC announces its decision on the ATV transmission standard.

Table 1.1—Milestones in High Definition Video Production

The Advanced Television Test Center was set up to manage the process of selecting a High Definition video transmission technology. Just before the final proposal submission deadline in June 1991, General Instrument announced that it had developed compression technology that enabled it to compress the bandwidth required for 6 NTSC channels into a single NTSC signal, and that this technique would work to compress an HDTV signal into a single NTSC channel. Within weeks, all of the other proponents, except for NHK (with Sony, one of the original partners in the development of HDTV), announced that they also had all-digital transmission schemes.

Early in 1993 it became clear that none of the proposed digital transmission schemes was demonstrably superior to any of the others. To forestall any protracted legal battles, each of the remaining proponents formed, in May 1993, what is known as the Grand Alliance. The goal of the Grand Alliance was to come up with a single transmission scheme that would incorporate the best technologies from each proposal.

At the time of this writing, the work of the Grand Alliance is complete. However, even with the formal recommendation of an ATV transmission standard by the Grand Alliance, and pending a formal adoption of a standard by the FCC, there are indications that the U.S. cable industry does not completely support the decision. One of the nation's largest cable system operators has publicly endorsed the system that was not selected. They did this for a variety of reasons, not the least of which is the claim that the format is better suited to a cable distribution system.

High Definition Video—What Is It, Anyway?

High Definition video is an imaging medium that merges the "you are there" quality of television with the color reproduction, widescreen aspect, and richness of detail previously associated only with film.

As was mentioned in the Preface, High Definition video is not the same thing as High Definition Television (HDTV). High Definition video refers to high-resolution, widescreen video in general. HDTV is just one format of High Definition video; MUSE is another. Contrary to widely-held belief, worldwide standards for HDTV production do exist. There are currently two worldwide production standards; analog SMPTE 240M and its digital counterpart, 260M. These two standards define what most people think of as HDTV, also known as 1125/60, a reference to its line and field count. (It's like calling NTSC 525/59.94 or referring to PAL as 625/50.)

An example of a High Definition video transmission standard is MUSE, which at the moment is used only in Japan. There is no MUSE production equipment—no cameras, VTRs, or editors (there are, however, MUSE videodisc players). Instead, material produced in 1125/60 HDTV gets converted to MUSE before it is broadcast (or, if produced in another format, gets transferred to 1125/60 and then gets converted to MUSE).

The distinction between production and transmission standards is an important one that often gets overlooked in conversations about the status of the selection of a U.S. High Definition video transmission standard. This distinction is covered later in this chapter.

A More Technical Look

The SMPTE standards, 240M and 260M, are based on work begun by NHK in the late 1960s, and they call for an image with an aspect ratio (shape) of 16:9, a line count of 1125 (of which 1035 are displayed), a count of 1920 (non-square) pixels per line, and a frame rate of exactly 30 frames/second (fps), interlaced (or, 60 fields/second).

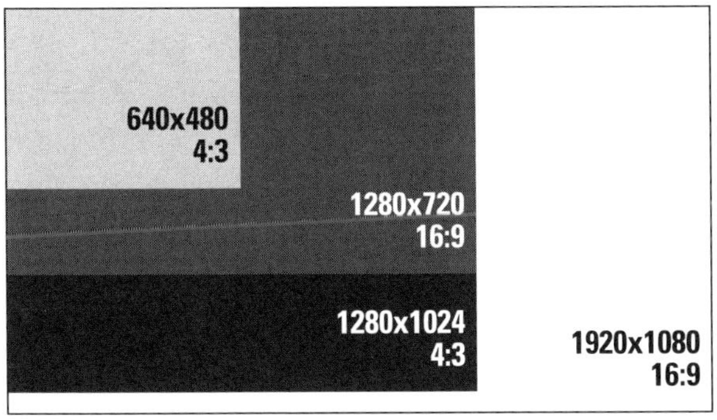

Figure 1.4—Relative image sizes

In computer terms, the SMPTE standards provide for an image with over six times the number of pixels as a 640 x 480 computer display; 2.5 times more pixels than 1024 x 768 computer displays; and 1.5 times more pixels than 1280 x 1024 computer displays.

Compared with the current U.S. broadcast practice (as defined by NTSC RS 170-A), SMPTE 240M and 260M are capable of recording more than five times the spatial information and more than three times the color information.

HDTV is the only commercially available imaging, recording, and reproduction system designed, from the outset, with end-to-end, consistent color reproduction in mind. HDTV was designed from the beginning to deliver representative color reproduction, what the SMPTE standards call metameric color reproduction. Briefly, this means that under conditions of equal color temperature illumination, the colors on the monitor will be the same as those in the scene in the front of the camera.

It is the combination of physical resolution and color rendition that causes people to remark that looking at an HDTV monitor is like "looking through a window."

What HDTV Is Not

It's NOT Just Television

The developers of HDTV had the right idea when they came up with the name Hi-Vision to describe their new high resolution video imaging system. By not using the word television, they sought to avoid many of the limiting connotations that the word carries. Unfortunately, the rest of the world did not take a page from this particular book when they chose the phrase High Definition Television to describe their new video systems.

The uses for High Definition video imaging systems go far beyond mere television (which is why we prefer to use the phrase High Definition video over High Definition Television). Think of all the places where fast, high quality, accurate color imaging can be useful, and you have a potential application for High Definition video imaging. There are uses for High Definition video everywhere that high quality "real" imagery is needed to aid communication and understanding, and not just in television.

It's NOT a Replacement for Film

When HDTV was introduced into the United States in the early to mid 1980s, proponents made the mistake of introducing it as a replacement for—not an alternative to—traditional film production. Now, almost a decade later, film producers are just beginning to fully appreciate the differences between High Definition video and film.

Still, for many clients, High Definition video is not an acceptable alternative to film. This is a subjective and aesthetic judgment as much as it is a technical one. Where some consider the sharpness and "television-ness" of High Definition video a drawback, others view it as a characteristic of the medium to be exploited, especially when using High Definition video matting and compositing for film special effects.

There are some aspects, however, of High Definition video that are remarkably like film. This is particularly true in terms of visual language, where the widescreen 16:9 aspect of HDTV requires a different eye for framing and camera movement than is developed for 4:3 video and film.

HDTV IS...

Its own medium—a unique combination of many of the best characteristics of video and film.

The Look of HD

One often asked question concerns how the 1125/60 format was arrived at. After all, it's not that much higher in resolution than conventional video, and it's certainly not as high resolution as 35mm film, the medium it was supposed to replace. The number of scanning lines was chosen as a result of extensive visual tests of projected film and video. While film is capable of much higher resolution than video, it is important to pay attention to resolution where it counts—on the screen.

A single frame of film that is not moving is capable of recording images at several thousand lines of resolution. The moment the film starts to move, however, the actual resolution drops. Each time a piece of film passes through a transport system, the resolution drops even more. This loss of resolution is made more apparent by the need to duplicate the film through optical printing mechanisms. Each time the film is duplicated, not only does it go through another transport system, but the copy is never an exact duplicate of the original. Detail and sharpness (resolution) are lost each step of the way. Even when digital techniques are used extensively in a film's production there are any number of mechanical transport steps and duplication steps between the camera negative and the release print. (See *Transferring High Definition Video to Film* on page 74.)

High Definition video, however, is not subject to the same losses in resolution due to mechanical transports. While there is some generational loss when creating multilayered effects using analog compositing equipment, it is possible to perform all effects completely in the digital domain.

By the time a film image reaches a theater screen via a projection system, the theoretical resolving power of film has dropped dramatically. A careful study of the actual resolution of film images when they reach the screen helped determine the resolution for HDTV. The goal was to create a system that could deliver at least the resolution of the average first-run film at the average multiplex. The net result of working completely in HDTV is a projected image capable of delivering more resolution to the screen of the average multiplex theater than 35mm film.

A tougher question concerns the debate over the aesthetic worth of the electronic look of High Definition video relative to the expressiveness and range of looks that film offers. There are no simple answers here. The best answer is that High Definition video extends the range of options open to filmmakers, offering a new tool that can be used to achieve a new range of looks. (See *John Alonzo, On Transferring High Definition Video to Film* on page 111.)

When considering this debate it's instructive to go back to the early days of film and to examine a similar controversy surrounding the introduction of sync sound. Originally, films were produced at 16 fps, resulting in a flickering picture even though each frame was projected twice. With the introduction of talkies, the frame rate was upped to 24 fps and this caused tremendous confusion. People had become accustomed to a visual language of film that included flickering. By any objective measure, 24 fps film was much better than 16 fps—there was much less flicker plus there was sync sound. But people had become used to the look and feel of projected 16 fps film with live music and many resisted the advance, saying that the 24 pictures per second looked 'unnatural.'

There's a similar 'unnatural' feeling about most computer graphics as well. This is because almost everything is in perfect focus and surfaces are usually blemish free. That's not the way things are in the real world; it's not what you're used to seeing, so it makes you uncomfortable and you usually don't know why. But you do know it doesn't look quite right.

There is something unnatural-looking about HDTV at first, too. It just doesn't look like anything else you've ever seen. For this reason, it takes some getting used to. And some people just don't like the look, or don't see that the image is any better.

When confronted with High Definition noninterlaced video, even experienced High Definition video watchers have remarked that the images don't look 'quite right.' The visual experience of High Definition, noninterlaced video is unlike anything else, and for that reason, it takes just as much getting used to as any other new medium.

Production Versus Transmission

It is necessary to understand that the focus of the FCC's efforts with respect to choosing a transmission standard is really about, "In what format should video be transmitted, assuming an antenna which is attached to a tower sitting on the ground?"

Before the formation of the Grand Alliance, there were a number of High Definition video production standards and transmission formats in existence worldwide, and a number of proposals vying to become the U.S. High Definition video terrestrial transmission standard.

The SMPTE 240M and 260M 1125/60 standards represent the only HDTV *production* standards in existence that are endorsed by a recognized international standards setting group. Program material produced in either of these formats is not directly broadcastable; it must be converted to another format for transmission. In Japan, this format is MUSE. The analog MUSE format is used for satellite transmission in Japan only, as well as for videodisc distribution.

Eureka is the name given to the European Community's efforts to develop its own High Definition video transmission format. As with SMPTE 240M HDTV, Eureka-formatted High Definition video must be converted to another format, for example HD-MAC (High Definition-Multiplexed Analog Component) for transmission.

The Grand Alliance's ATV proposal only specifies how High Definition video is to be transmitted, not how it must be produced. Material that is produced according to the SMPTE 240M HDTV standard could be transmitted via ATV. Theoretically, NTSC, PAL, SECAM, and Eureka can also be transmitted via ATV.

Two good analogies that illustrate the difference between production and transmission are film and D1 video. Film is used to produce a lot of television programs and movies, but the film itself is not directly transmittable. It must first be converted, using a telecine, into an electronic form—NTSC, PAL, or SECAM—in order to be transmitted.

D1 is a little closer to the production/transmission pathway of High Definition video, because it starts out as video, comes from a component camera, is usually originally recorded in a different medium (for example, Betacam), and then gets transferred to D1 for editing. Like film, D1 video itself is not directly transmittable. No form of component video, analog or digital, is. D1 video must first be converted to composite NTSC, PAL, or SECAM video in order to be transmitted.

It is important to note once again that selection of an ATV format will only govern the transmission—not the production—of High Definition video. At the present, no production infrastructure exists to create programming in any of the ATV formats. Therefore, 1125/60 will likely be supported at least until ATV compatible, competitive production technologies can be made commercially viable.

Advanced Television (ATV)

The production/transmission dichotomy will still exist for some time with ATV because, at present, there isn't any production or postproduction equipment that adheres to any of the ATV formats.

ATV should make things a little easier, however, by supporting a number of different image formats; it won't be locked into the 1920 pixel by 1125 line interlaced HDTV specification. ATV supports two different high-resolution image formats, 1280 by 720 pixels and 1920 by 1080 pixels; three different scanning frequencies, 60, 30, and 24 Hz; square pixels; and both noninterlaced and interlaced scanning. Interlaced (60 field) scanning is supported only at 1920 by 1080 resolution.

The mechanism for supporting ATV's multiple formats—all of which share the widescreen 16:9 aspect ratio selected for HDTV—will digitize and packetize the video and audio signals before transmitting them. Each packet, or chunk, of digital data begins with what is referred to as a "header descriptor block." This header descriptor block contains information that describes not only the format, but also the type and content of the information that follows.

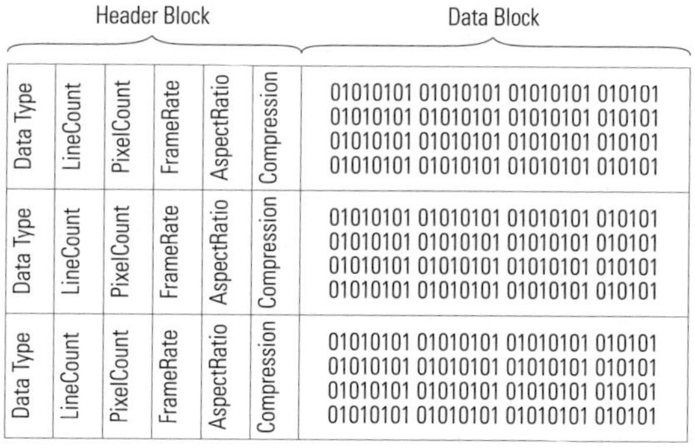

Figure 1.5—ATV header descriptor block schematic

ATV receivers will, in all likelihood, end up being sophisticated image processing engines with frame memory and dedicated decompression circuitry capable of decoding these "header descriptor blocks" and properly displaying the data that follows. The capabilities of the ATV receiver itself will probably be limited only by the amount of money a viewer wishes to spend.

Attached to the output of the ATV receiver will be the equivalent of a digital multistandard monitor capable of displaying whatever type of image the ATV receiver can output. For example, an ATV receiver might be able to receive and decode all of the ATV formats, but only have the memory and display circuitry to output images at 'standard' (526 or 625) resolution. However, by buying additional frame memory and more powerful processor cards, viewers would be able to upgrade the capabilities of their ATV system incrementally.

Finally, the ATV header descriptor blocks are being designed so that they can, theoretically anyway, support all sorts of image formats and technologies not yet invented. This means that

ATV receivers can be designed to support programming produced in formats that the ATV standard does not now support.

These are just a few of the advantages to be gained by moving away from analog to digital transmission technologies. By carefully designing an open system that can be modified relatively easily to take advantages of new technologies as they are developed, the whole issue of completely changing the television system may never arise again.

Chapter 2

Video For Poets

The traditional purpose of a video system is to move images from one place to another over a wire, or to record an image for playback at a later time. In order to do this, three basic technologies are required:

1 A technique for converting various intensities of light to electrical impulses—which is done using a camera;

2 A technique for converting the electrical impulses back to light—which is done using a television or monitor; and

3 A technique for recording electrical impulses and playing them back—which is done using a videotape recorder, or VTR.

Although the techniques are few and easy to enumerate, translating them into a working system involves many complex technical details. In this chapter, several of the techniques are reviewed as a base for understanding how these ideas translate into High Definition video and how they end up having an impact on production and engineering.

A Short Historical Introduction to Color TV

The various technologies of black-and-white television were invented and refined during the 1930s, with the first television broadcast taking place during the New York World's Fair in 1939. When the FCC began to investigate adding color to television broadcasts in the 1950s, they decided that whatever system was adopted for transmitting the color television signal must be compatible with the existing installed base of black-and-white receivers in American homes. Thus, to a large extent, the NTSC (National Television Standards Committee) system now in use in the United States, Japan, and other countries is based on the capabilities and limitations of technologies now almost 60 years old.

The choice of aspect ratio for television goes back even further. When the original black-and-white television format was being developed, the inventors looked around for a large source of existing programming material. What else would they choose but 16mm films—which just happened to have an aspect ratio of 4:3? Thus, one of the main reasons for television looking the way it does is based on decisions made for film around 100 years ago.

Note

Body text in this chapter that is set in **bold** type indicates that there is an entry in the Glossary, (Chapter 9) for that word or phrase.

Cameras

Tube cameras accomplish their task by scanning the light striking a photosensitive tube. The scanning process, which happens at a constant rate, converts what is essentially a parallel data stream (all of the light strikes the tube simultaneously) into a serial data stream.

Light striking the face of the tube is converted into electrical impulses in proportion to the intensity of that light. An electron beam scanning the inside face of the tube senses the different light levels, converting them into a stream of electrical voltages. The light striking the tube appears **analog** in nature. That is, the intensity levels are infinitely—and smoothly—variable, not changeable only in discrete steps. The stream of voltages generated by the scanning beam also appears analog in nature and exhibits the same infinite variability.

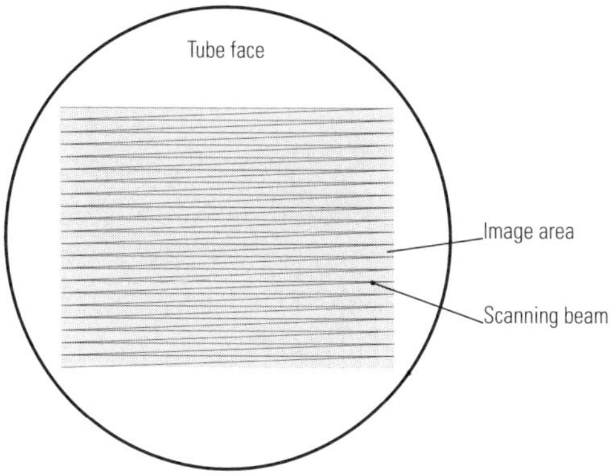

Figure 2.1—Scanning the Tube Face

To create high quality color images, the light entering the camera is split into three paths using a prism. These three light beams are passed through colored filters that pass only one color of light. These three light beams then strike separate photosensitive tubes, each one generating a stream of voltages. These voltage streams are not color in themselves. Rather, they represent the red, green, and blue color information in the scene as separate monochrome images. The **resolution** (see *Resolution* on page 24) of the image is partly a function of the area of the tube that is scanned, and partly the size and speed of the scanning electron beam.

In a CCD or chip camera, the process is similar, except that instead of the light striking tubes, the three beams of light strike electronic CCD chips. The chip is scanned serially, generating an analog voltage stream. The resolution of the image is partly a function of the size of the chip, and partly the number and size of the individual sensors (**pixels**) on the chip. Other factors, including the quality of the lens on the camera, also affect resolution. The output of most chip cameras is an analog signal. Only later on, in the camera's CCU or in a digital VTR, are the analog signals **digitized** and recorded on tape as digital data. (In a Sony Digital Betacam camera, the signal is digitized right after the CCD.)

The Structure of the Picture (Lines and Fields and Frames [Oh, My!]).

Video images are composed of a sequence of still images. Each image is called a *frame.* In order to reduce the amount of information that needs to be sent, as well as to increase the quality of motion at low frame rates, the frames are divided into two *fields*, one containing the odd numbered lines, the other containing the even numbered lines. The method of combining the two fields into one frame is called **interlacing**. NTSC, PAL, SECAM, and HDTV all use this technique, and so they are called *interlaced video.*

The smoothness of motion in an image is determined in part by the number of different still pictures presented each second. For example, film presents 24 frames per second (fps); NTSC, 59.94 fields (29.97 frames); PAL, 50 fields (25 frames); SMPTE 240M HDTV, 60 fields (30 frames); and Eureka (1250/50) 50 fields (25 frames).

There is also a method of displaying a video picture which does not use interlacing. When all the lines in the picture, odd and even, are sequentially drawn creating a complete frame, the technique is called **progressive** scanning or **noninterlaced** scanning. All other things being equal, progressive scanning requires double the bandwidth for the same spatial resolution as an interlaced picture.

In general, interlaced scanning is good for motion imagery, combining high perceived resolution for moving objects with relatively low bandwidth requirements. Progressive scanning, which is the technique used in most computer monitors, works well when there are large amounts of text and/or when there is relatively little motion in a scene.

Perhaps more importantly, progressively scanned video is easier to transfer to film than interlaced video because the image does not have to be de-interlaced for 30 to 24 frame rate conversion. The proposed ATV transmission standard encourages progressive scanning as a preferred display format.

Frame Rates

Black-and-white TV originally had a field rate of exactly 60 per second. This rate was chosen because of the vagaries of 1930's power supply technology: 60 Hz alternating current was what came out of American wall sockets. When NTSC color was being developed in the 1950s, the field rate was changed slightly to 59.94 (1/10 of 1% difference) to reduce picture interference caused by the color and sound subcarriers. As you might imagine, this very slight difference in frame rates caused some problems in the early days of NTSC production. The twinned concepts of drop frame timecode and nondrop frame timecode evolved to address these problems.

The need to address these issues continues today in High Definition video production, which, like the original black-and-white TV, is exactly 30 frames per second. Accommodating the differences in frame rates is now well understood, and while modern offline and online editing systems can be set to compensate for the program length differences between drop frame and nondrop frame timecode—solving all postproduction frame rate issues—there is still a need to deal with these differences when integrating High Definition video with NTSC in live production situations. (For a more in-depth discussion of frame rate conversion issues, see *High Definition/Standard Definition Compatibility Issues* beginning on page 62. For a more in-depth discussion of High Definition video/standard definition integration issues, see *Woodstock '94: Live Multicamera Production Integrating High Definition Video and NTSC* beginning on page 100.)

The Importance of Sync

There are a lot of components in video systems: cameras, VTRs, monitors, switchers, effects devices, etc. In order for all these devices to display the same image at the same time it is necessary to synchronize them by providing them with a common point of reference with respect to the beginning of each new field and line. This is done by providing **sync** pulses with the video signals. There are two types of sync pulses, horizontal and vertical.

In some cases, the sync information is a part of the video signal; at other times, sync is carried on a separate wire. The video part of the signal describes the visual image; the sync part of the signal is not visible. Sync pulses describe where frames start and end. In order to combine different video sources, the frames from each source need to start and end at the same time relative to each other. The process of synchronizing the start and end times of two or more video sources is called **genlocking**.

Sync pulses in NTSC are referred to as bi-level because they are composed of two voltage levels. HDTV equipment uses tri-level sync, as can be seen in Figure 2.2. When comparing the SMPTE 240M tri-level video signal to NTSC, there are a number of differences to be aware of.

1 There is no black pedestal. The video signal can range from 0 to 700 mv.

2 There is no subcarrier/burst information in the signal. The original 5:3 aspect ratio HDTV bi-level sync signal did have burst information in it, but it was used for internal equipment timing, not color encoding. The tri-level sync signal was designed to provide more stable genlocking using a narrower **blanking** interval.

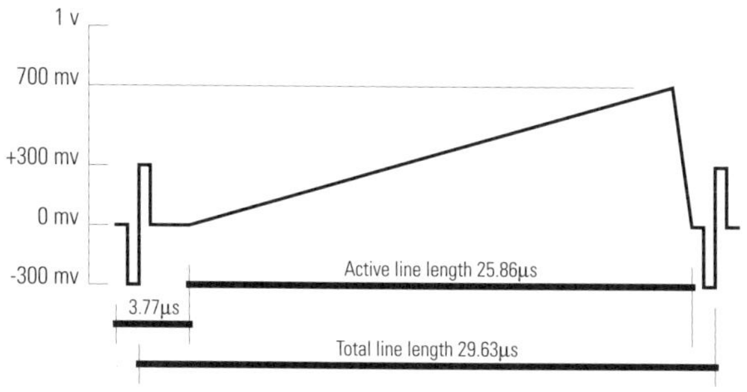

Figure 2.2—SMPTE 240M HDTV tri-level sync signal schematic

The Difference Between Composite and Component Video

One of the most difficult tasks facing the original designers of color television was to figure out how to devise a color signal that could also be received on a black-and-white set. They did this by initially recognizing that color images can be thought of as being composed of three monochrome images, called **components**. Each of these component images represent the color information in the scene in front of the camera. Through calculation or filtering, a single image is created that contains most of the picture information in black-and-white. This is called the **luminance** (brightness) signal. The image in the luminance signal (which is the image displayed on a black-and-white television set) consists mostly of information from the green component of the picture, because green light contains the most energy. Additional calculations or filtering is performed that results in separate, highly compressed color, or **chrominance** signals.

There are several mathematical formulas used to calculate luminance and chrominance. In NTSC the formula is called YIQ. In Betacam the formula is called Y, R minus Y, B minus Y. In HDTV the formula is called **YPbPr**. All three formulas perform essentially the same task, **compression**, effectively reducing the amount of redundant information in the video signal.

By reversing the calculations, or filtering, it is possible to recreate the original color picture quite accurately. The process of converting component **RGB** (referred to as **GBR** in High Definition video) to another form of component video is sometimes referred to as **color space** conversion.

When the luminance image and the chrominance signals are combined into a single electrical signal the result is called **composite** video. In this case, composite video refers to a method of combining the original components

(RGB; Y, R minus Y, B minus Y; etc.) into one video signal. The device that combines the separate components is called an **encoder**. NTSC is a form of composite video, as are PAL and SECAM. Color composite video is characterized by its ability to fit on a single wire.

When the RGB or luminance and chrominance information is distributed, processed, and recorded separately, the result is called component video. In most cases (for example Betacam) the luminance and chrominance components are what get recorded. This is also the case with High Definition video—the video is always in a component format; *there is no such thing as composite High Definition video*, and this is one of the reasons High Definition video looks so good.

Most (but not all) High Definition video equipment is capable of generating, converting, and/or recording both YPbPr and GBR component video. Because of this, it is important to check all of the ins and outs to make sure that if, for example, the camera is generating GBR, that the device connected to the camera expects to see GBR. Getting this mixed up is unfixable.

Every High Definition VTR records component YPbPr video, even though it might accept GBR as input and be able to output GBR. Only rarely in television systems are GBR components recorded. However, RGB components are routinely used in computer graphics systems.

The process of combining the luminance and chrominance channels is imperfect and causes considerable distortion in the resulting composite video signal. It is possible to convert composite video back into its component parts, but the resulting image is never as good as the original component image. A device that converts composite video into component video is called a **decoder**. A device that converts one form of component video into another form of component video is called a **transcoder**.

The Differences Between Analog and Digital

Analog signals are continuously variable with an infinite number of possible values between minimum and maximum. The curve in Figure 2.3 is representative of what an analog signal looks like. If we were able to zoom in closer and closer, the smoothness of the curve wouldn't change; it isn't possible, ever, to discern discrete steps.

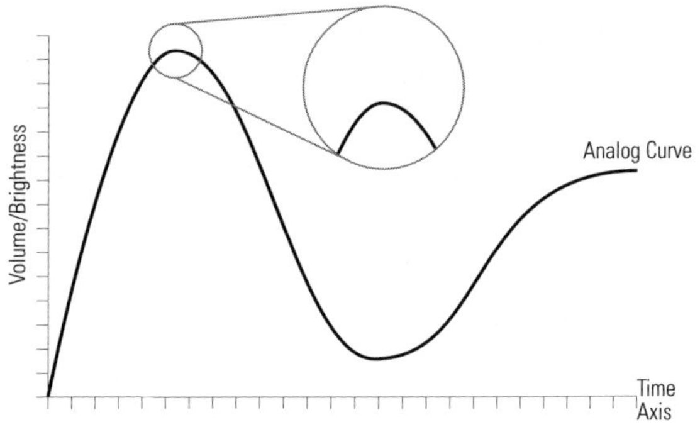

Figure 2.3—Analog signal

Two factors determine the quality of the digitized signal. For each unit of time (called the **sample** rate) the height of the curve is measured, or sampled. The quality of the data that is sampled—its precision—is determined by the number of **bits** used. The sample rate and precision determine the resolution of the sampling grid.

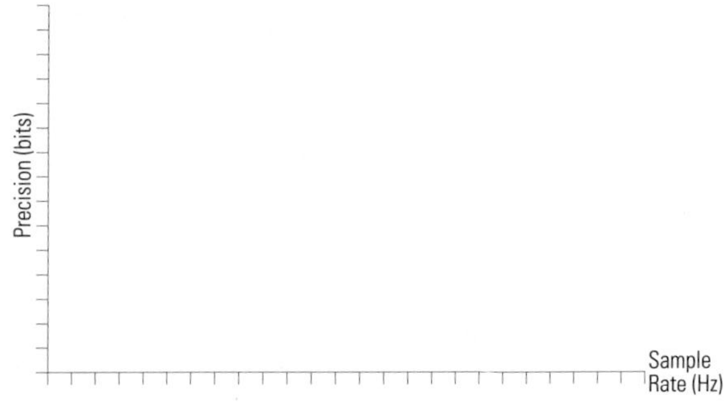

Figure 2.4—Sample rate and precision determine resolution

Fewer samples per second and fewer bits of precision result in a coarser sampling grid, making it difficult to reproduce the analog signal accurately.

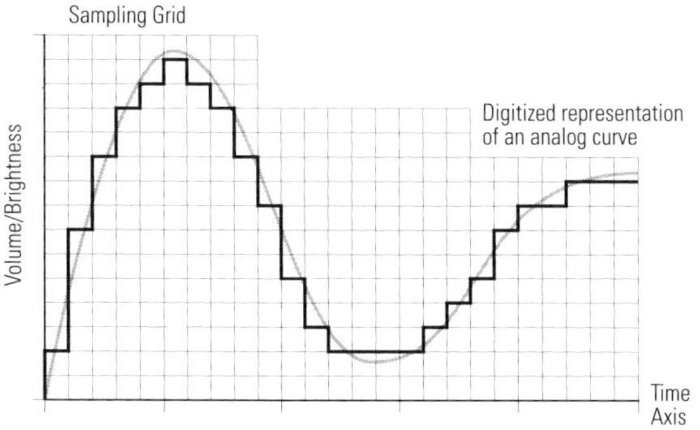

Figure 2.5—Low-resolution digital representation of an analog signal

Better results can be achieved—the curve can be more closely approximated—by increasing the sample rate and the number of bits of precision.

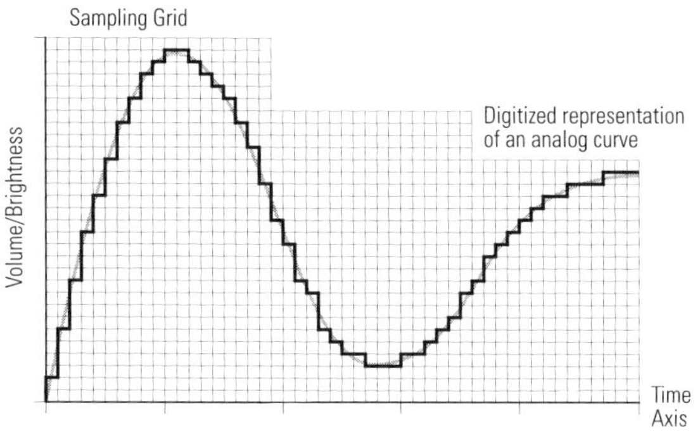

Figure 2.6—Higher-resolution digital representation of the same analog signal

What gets recorded on tape is the height of the curve, which is represented by a series of numbers or codes. Because only the height of the curve is recorded at each moment in time, it is impossible to know what is actually happening to the curve between samples. When reproducing the recording, sophisticated filtering is performed on the samples to help smooth the curve.

Theoretically, analog systems should produce better results than digital systems because there is no loss of data through digitizing (or quantizing). In practice, however, digital systems are more robust. Because digital systems record the sampled codes, they are less susceptible to data loss and degradation through multiple generations of recording and playback.

There are theoretical considerations and practical upper limits that determine the minimum and maximum resolution of the sampling grid. A mathematician named **Nyquist** proved that it is only necessary to sample the data at twice the maximum frequency that needs to be reproduced accurately.

With audio, for example, the sampling rate of audio CDs is set at 44.1 kHz, in part because the human ear can rarely hear above 20 kHz, and in part, because of the capacity of the CD itself. Other sampling rates are used, however. A rate of 48 kHz is used in High Definition VTRs while 22 and 11 kHz, and lower, are used to compress the audio signal in many computer applications to save space. In general, 16 bits (>64,000 steps) of precision are used to measure the height of the curve, though 18-bit, 20-bit, and greater resolutions are used in some professional applications, and 8-bit and 4-bit are used in some computer applications.

In standard definition video, the data is sampled at a rate based on a fundamental frequency, called subcarrier. Usually luminance is sampled at 4x subcarrier, and chrominance at 2x subcarrier. This results in digital video being characterized as 4:2:2. In 4:4:4 systems all of the components are sampled at 4x subcarrier. Alpha (key or mask) channels can also be included in this notation scheme; common examples are 4:2:2:4 and 4:4:4:4. Video images are typically sampled with 8 bits (256 levels) of precision, but 10 bits (1024 levels) are becoming increasingly common. The SMPTE 260M digital High Definition video specification supports both 8- and 10-bit sampling.

For comparison purposes, high-end color prepress systems routinely sample at 12 bits (4096 levels) per RGB component, and 16-bit systems are becoming increasingly common. Also, 8 bits per color has been shown to be adequate to acceptably reproduce most images on paper; the additional color information is designed to compensate for nonlinearities and the inevitable mathematical round-off errors that creep in during multigeneration, digital image processing. Losing the least significant bit due to round-off in an 8-bit system reduces the number of meaningful information levels by half—from 256 to 128. Losing the four least significant bits from a 16-bit system still leaves 4096 levels that contain meaningful color information.

Resolution

Resolution is a measure of the ability of a system to resolve detail. Higher resolution systems are able to capture, record, and display more detail than lower resolution systems.

In television systems, resolution is measured by pointing a camera at a specially designed test chart or pattern or by using a machine to electronically generate the chart. These test charts are images consisting mainly of patterns of black-and-white lines that get progressively closer and closer together. Each pair of black lines is separated by a white space. If it is possible to see the white spaces between the lines, then the camera and monitor combination (and if the image is recorded, the VTR as well) can be said to resolve that many TV lines (TVL—not to be confused with scanning lines).

The ability of a television system to resolve detail is based on a lot of factors, including the quality of the lens, whether or not there are filters in front of the lens, the size of the scanning target, the size of the electron beam scanning the target, the size of the individual pixels on the CCD chip, and whether or not the image or signal is compressed or encoded, among other factors.

When NTSC was developed in the mid 1950s, there were no digital pictures. Therefore, the resolution of NTSC images was not defined in terms of a pixel grid.

The NTSC format specifies 525 scanning lines per frame, of which 483 are active (that is, they contain picture information). The scan rate is 59.94 fields/second. There is no direct specification of the number of pixels per line in NTSC.

In most PC-based computer graphics systems, the resolution of NTSC images has been fixed at 480 lines of 640 pixels. This results in square pixels, which reduces the amount of calculating the computer has to do to generate images (circles especially) with the correct aspect ratio. But video has never relied on square pixels, and both D1 (at 720 by 484 pixels) and D2 (at 768 by 484 pixels) eschew them. (Before inexpensive **antialiasing** techniques were introduced, character generators routinely used to pack a lot of very, very skinny pixels onto each line to reduce jagged edges and to make small type legible.)

The 480 line count that originated with PC-based computer graphics systems is actually 3 lines short of the active line count of NTSC video. However, these lines are in the **overscan** area of the picture and are rarely, if ever, seen on a standard consumer TV set.

Bandwidth and Compression

The term **bandwidth** is used to refer to the amount of information contained in a signal. The more information in a signal, the greater the amount of bandwidth required to encode the information. Bandwidth is often measured in MHz (megahertz, or cycles per second) and in MB/s (megabytes per second).

Compression refers to techniques used to reduce the amount of bandwidth a signal requires. In general, there are two kinds of compression: **lossless**, in which it is possible to exactly reconstruct the original signal from the compressed signal, and **lossy**, in which information is irretrievably thrown away during the compression process.

A single 1125/60 HDTV image is composed of 1035 active (viewable) horizontal lines with 1920 pixels per line, resulting in a total of 1,987,200 pixels per frame or, at 30 frames per second, approximately 60 million pixels per second.

High Definition video production systems convert the GBR signal generated in the camera head into YPbPr (the HDTV video luminance (Y) and chrominance (Pb, Pr) components), during which redundant information in the original component GBR signals is thrown away. (The conversion process can be done in the camera head, in the CCU, or in the VTR.) At this point, while there is a fair amount of compression, it is, practically speaking, lossless.

In a Sony HDD–1000 digital VTR, the component signals are then sampled; the luminance component at full bandwidth (30 MHz) and the two chrominance components at half bandwidth (15 MHz)—or 4:2:2. (Other VTRs sample the GBR to YPbPr at different rates, see Table 4.4 on page 52.) This subsampling of the chrominance signals is an example of lossy compression. Information has been thrown away irretrievably. However, the information that is being thrown away has been carefully chosen so that it has little visual effect on the picture.

If there were no color space conversion from GBR to YPbPr and subsampling of the two chrominance channels, the video data rate would be 180 MB/second, not including error correction coding (**ECC**) data (see *Error Correction Coding (ECC) and Concealment* on page 26). Through color space conversion and subsampling the image data rate in a digital VTR is reduced to 120 MB/s, plus ECC. For comparison purposes, the 8 CD-quality audio channels that the Sony HD–1000 VTR is capable of recording require only about 1.25 MB/s for all eight channels. In UNIHI VTRs, which record analog signals, the data rate is further reduced by limiting the bandwidth—and consequently the resolution—to 20 MHz for luminance and 7 MHz for each of the chrominance channels.

At the time of writing, the only forms of compression used in High Definition video production equipment are color space conversion and subsampling. The next generation of equipment, however, will use additional compression steps to further reduce the amount of data actually being recorded on the VTR in order to make cameras and VTRs more portable and less expensive. The approaches that are being suggested (MPEG2 is an example) are similar to the ones being used in transmission systems to make High Definition video fit into the bandwidth of an NTSC channel.

There are a lot of opinions on the problems that using a variety of compression schemes will introduce into the production, postproduction, and distribution of all forms of digital video, whether High Definition or standard definition. The problems are very real, and at the moment, no one has any idea what the ultimate impact cascading more or less compatible compression schemes will have on image quality. (For a more technical discussion of compression, see *Compression* on page 147.)

Getting it on Tape

To accomplish the feat of recording over 120 MB of data per second on 1" digital tape, several things have been done. The first is that the tape is extremely thin; a one-hour reel of High

Definition digital tape has more than three times more tape on it than a one-hour reel of 1" Type-C tape. Second, the tape is pulled through the machine comparatively quickly. Finally, the tape is recorded using a very common technique called helical-scan recording.

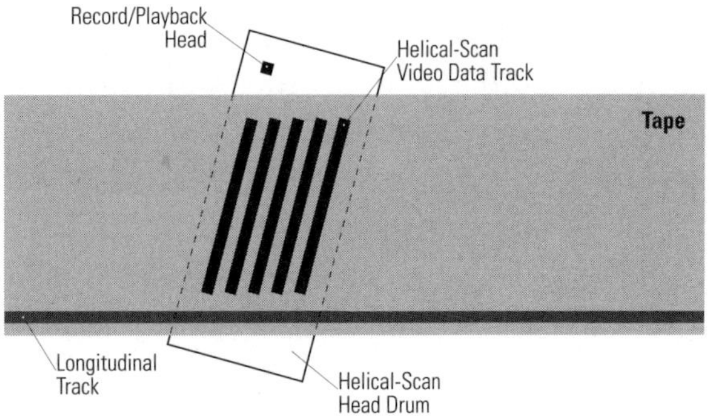

Figure 2.7—Helical-scan drum head

In helical-scan recording, the head rotating drum is situated at an angle to the tape. The spinning heads record parallel slices of video information on the tape instead of longitudinally (along the length of the tape), as seen in Figure 2.7. The Sony HDD–1000 VTR has eight video heads, and the record and error correction circuitry are designed in such a way that even if one of the heads were to fail completely, it would still be possible to record to, and play back from, the VTR.

In addition to more efficiently utilizing the amount of space on the tape by many orders of magnitude, helical-scan recording also increases the effective head to tape speed, which increases the recording density, and consequently the signal to noise ratio and bandwidth—resolution.

The effective head to tape speed in a Sony HDD–1000 digital High Definition VTR is about 120 m.p.h. or over 2100 inches per second. By way of comparison, a high quality analog open reel audio tape recorder, which records longitudinally with fixed heads, has a maximum head to tape speed of 30 inches per second.

Error Correction Coding (ECC) and Concealment

In every robust digital recording scheme, redundancy is built into the data that gets recorded in order to make it possible to reconstruct bad or missing data in the case of partial tape or head failure. High Definition digital VTRs are no exception to this rule, and because of the huge amounts of data involved, ECC is especially important. Table 2.1 helps demonstrate the concept of ECC. It is not the exact scheme employed in a digital VTR.

a	b	c	a+b+c
d	e	f	d+e+f
g	h	i	g+h+i
a+d+g	b+e+h	c+f+i	a+e+i

Table 2.1—Error correction coding example

For each block of pixels (a 3 by 3 block size is used for this example; in practice, additional checksums are also calculated and recorded) a number of checksums are generated. By adding up the values of individual pixels and comparing the result with the checksums, the value for each pixel can be verified. In the event that the numbers disagree, additional calculations are performed and their checksums are compared. Through this process, it is possible to derive the correct values for bad pixels. One advantage of the way ECC is implemented in digital VTRs is that when a tape is digitally dubbed, bad or missing pixels can be replaced with the correct or missing values.

Sometimes errors are so extensive that they cannot be corrected. In these cases, the VTR **conceals** them by attempting to recreate the value of the bad pixels by examining pixels in the immediate vicinity. Unlike corrected errors, concealed errors are never really fixed; they just get hidden. However, concealment is so good that often even a professional eye can't notice the conceals, and if it weren't for the fact that the VTR keeps track of them (the display indicates the number of conceals and their timecode locations), you'd never know that they were there. The concealment algorithms are powerful enough to compensate for the loss or damage of a head on the drum. However, if this were to happen, the conceal would almost certainly be visible in most program material.

Image Quality

There are many factors that go into determining the quality of an image—many of them subjective, many objective. If the factor can be measured on a scope and compared against a reference standard, then it is objective. If the factor can only be determined by eye, then it is subjective.

Measures of quality are never absolute. Instead, quality needs to be measured against the technical and visual requirements of a particular project. For example, one measure of image quality is resolution. However, the optical qualities of a lens ultimately determines the quality of the image reaching the sensor—whether CCD or tube. It doesn't matter how good the sensor is, if the lens distorts or otherwise affects the image. It is the balance of all of the factors affecting image quality within the confines of a budget that determines what is appropriate quality for a given project. (See *Transferring High Definition Video to Film* beginning on page 74.)

Chapter 3 Production

> "A word to the wise. The old NTSC attitude, 'We'll fix it in post,' can come back to haunt you in HD. It's better to get it right when you shoot it—even if it costs more—because it will almost certainly cost even more to fix it in post—*if* it can be fixed at all."
>
> —*Anonymous HDTV producer*

Virtually all productions require that compromises be made during preproduction to match the project's requirement to the available budget. These compromises are inevitable. Ultimately the trade-off is, "How much needs to be spent to achieve the desired look and level of quality?"

For much of the first decade of High Definition video production, these compromises were very, very real given the scarcity of equipment and its level of development. Since the introduction of the UNIHI format and smaller ENG-style cameras, however, many of the limitations that forced substantial compromises have disappeared for a large number of shooting situations.

The quote that begins this chapter is very much a relic of the early days of HDTV production. Nowadays, it is possible to fix just about everything in post. You may not be able to fix it using a piece of equipment that operates in real time, and it will probably cost a bit, but it can be fixed. That does not mean, however, that a High Definition video producer, director, DP, camera operator, or engineer can relax during production. It's *always* better to get it right the first time.

The purpose of this chapter is to provide you with an understanding of the issues REBO producers face each time they start production on a High Definition video project and that need to be dealt with in order to be able to answer the question, "What equipment is right for the creative and technical requirements of the job and the budget?"

Production issues are also discussed in Chapter 6, *Case Studies*, and Chapter 7, *Creative Considerations.*

Keys to Successful High Definition Video Production

1 To paraphrase a famous comedian, "Preproduction! Preproduction! Preproduction!"

2 Successful High Definition video producers and production companies recognize that they must act in an educational and liaison capacity, communicating to the client what the equipment is, and is not, easily capable of achieving.

3 Many things are going to take longer than they do in standard definition video.

While it used to be common for the director or DP to wait for engineering during a High Definition video production, with the most recent generation of equipment this is true less often than it used to be. Still, what seem like relatively simple tasks can take as long as they do in film production in part because of the bulk of the equipment and cabling, and in part because of the quality of the format (see point 4). It is important to schedule accordingly.

4 When it comes to production values, think film, not video.

The higher image quality of High Definition video means that many of the tricks that work in traditional video will no longer work. Set, costume, makeup, and lighting details that would be invisible in NTSC or PAL are often glaringly obvious in High Definition video, and more time (and money) is required to ensure that all of those details are dealt with appropriately.

It's also wise to keep in mind that High Definition video has many of the characteristics of film and it is worthwhile thinking about treating it like film for many projects. For example, lens filtration is less frequently considered in standard definition video.

5 Because High Definition video production equipment still hasn't reached the stage of development of standard definition video equipment, and because of its high image quality, the technical and engineering demands are correspondingly higher than they are in standard definition video production.

6 At the time of this writing, there is no such thing as a High Definition video camcorder. This means that you will *always* be shooting with an umbilical cord connecting the camera to an outboard VTR.

Figure 3.1—Tethered to engineering by an umbilical

These days, most films are shot with some sort of cable attached to the camera, for video assist for example, so the camera cable probably won't affect film crews as much because they are used to working with cameras that have cables. The video camera operator used to using a camcorder will have more problems getting used to having their movements limited by a camera cable.

Preproduction

An important phase (some think *the* most important phase) in all productions, whether film, standard definition video, or High Definition video, is preproduction.

It is during the preproduction phase that a project's creative concepts are reviewed and broken down into the myriad practical details required to capture the footage that meets the project brief. Many factors are evaluated during preproduction that ultimately determine the mix of equipment and the approach that gets used. The thoroughness and accuracy of the work everyone does during preproduction—often, actually, a matter of guessing right more often than wrong—determines, in no small measure, the eventual success of the final product. And that is also true in High Definition video.

The Preproduction Process

There are many reasons why projects get produced the way they do. Money is only one, but often it is the most important variable in the equation.

At REBO, the entire production process begins when a producer is assigned a project to produce. Often, the idea for the program is not completely worked out, and there might not even be a firm notion of the amount of money available to produce the project. In many cases this is because many clients aren't really sure what High Definition video is capable of, how it can be used most effectively, or how much it costs compared with film or standard definition video production.

REBO producers regularly find that the first task of preproduction is to work with clients to educate them about what High Definition video does best, most easily, and least expensively, in order to make sure that the client is getting the most program they can for the money they have to spend.

Depending on an assessment of the scope of the project, this initial creative development stage of preproduction may involve not only the producer, but more often than not, at least one engineer. If the client's creative idea is not well defined, then a DP, an editor, and/or an effects designer may also get involved.

As preproduction unfolds and alternatives are explored, the budget changes, and often, so does the project itself. A particular production method may suggest a change in creative content or artistic direction. Often, an effect can be achieved more effectively using a production technique that takes specific advantage of High Definition video.

Another important part of preproduction is to develop contingency plans in case something changes during production, including bad weather and equipment breaking down. Whatever might reasonably be expected to happen, needs to be planned for. This is also the case with traditional production, but the lack of easy access to backup gear makes this aspect of preproduction especially important for High Definition video production.

Personnel

When you get right down to it, there are very few major differences between the kind of crew required to shoot in High Definition video and those for film or standard definition video. There are several important differences however:

1 Every crew needs to include an engineer.

   The engineer's role is to ensure the quality of the shoot. A High Definition video project lives and dies by the quality of its engineering during production, and depends on the quality of the working relationship between the engineer and the Director and DP.

The engineer acts as an additional set of eyes and ears for the Director and DP, reviewing the camera image on a monitor, checking for correct exposure, color balance, video problems, audio levels, and a myriad of other details. Like many skills, it doesn't take very long to get the basics down, but it does take practice and experience until all the little details become second nature.

2 Camera operators should have some experience shooting widescreen.

There are subtle but obvious differences in framing and camera movement between the narrow 4:3 format of standard definition video, and High Definition video's widescreen 16:9 format. Like the engineering tasks, it takes practice to get proficient at seeing and working in widescreen.

For example, the camera operator just can't shoot a little wide, and frame everything up using a digital effects device in post, as might be done in NTSC. Digital effects devices for High Definition video are rare and expensive at the moment.

Also, the widescreen aspect ratio makes it possible to think of the frame in terms of thirds, not halves. This means that the director and camera operator don't need to center everything up in the frame. Two-shots can be a lot more interesting. Scenes can be framed a little wider to provide context.

3 The director needs to be aware of how the widescreen format affects shot design and selection, especially if the program material has to be 'protected' for 4:3 down-conversion.

Because of the amount of detail in each frame, and the shape of the frame, it is not necessary to cut nearly as fast as in 4:3 standard definition video.

When shooting for 16:9 and 4:3 simultaneously, some compromises obviously have to be made between the two. Which format is more important for release should ultimately determine which aspect ratio gets favored.

Because there is no portable camcorder yet, there are no one person crews in High Definition video. At a minimum, a crew will consist of four people: the director, the camera operator, the engineer, and the audio person. The standard crew REBO fields for EFP-style documentary productions consists of twice that number of people: director, line producer, camera operator/DP, engineer, audio person, grip, gaffer, and at least one PA. Everyone does more than one job.

For more discussion of crew requirements, refer to *New York: On The Edge* beginning on page 98, *Woodstock '94: Live Multicamera Production Integrating High Definition Video and NTSC* beginning on page 100, and *John Alonzo* beginning on page 109.

Equipment Availability

Unfortunately, there's just not a whole lot of High Definition video equipment around in the United States, and you just can't go to any old film or video rental house and get the equipment you need.

A large multicamera shoot can literally require all the equipment available in North America. If your production is scheduled at the same time, you may have to live with a less than perfect lens selection, not enough tape stock, or inadequate backup support in case a piece of equipment goes down.

For example, during a REBO shoot in western Mexico, a prototype of the Panasonic AK-HC900 camera—one of only two or three handbuilt prototypes in the world—fizzled blue smoke and stopped working. Fortunately, the manual was packed with the camera; unfortunately, it was in Japanese. Working over a cellular phone hookup through a translator to an engineer in Japan, the engineer on the shoot was able to determine what part fizzled. Luckily, it was just a burnt out resistor, and it would be possible to fix the camera and continue the shoot. But there aren't many electronic parts shops in small towns in western Mexico. Eventually, a portable radio was taken apart, and the necessary resistor was found and the fix was made.

During the 1994 Super Bowl, one of the engineers from NHK dropped a board from a camera he was working on, on the AstroTurf and shorted it out. The producer got on the phone from Atlanta, and late that night, was finally able to locate someone from Sony's emergency parts service at home who agreed to go back to the office and check the stock. Fortunately, there was a part to be had, and it was shipped by air the next morning, arriving in time for the game. This may not seem like such a problem until you consider that there were only four High Definition video cameras on site for the shoot. Losing one meant only having three, which would have made covering the game even more difficult. When you've got more than 20 NTSC cameras on a shoot, losing one doesn't have nearly the same impact.

Logistics and Transportation

Logistics and transportation are just two of the interesting problems when shooting in High Definition video, especially when traveling to remote locations. In these situations you have to take everything with you: there's no specialty rental house around the corner to pop into to get a replacement part or a special lens. It's often difficult enough just to get a primary piece of equipment, let alone adequate backup.

Weight, size, and special location requirements like a helicopter or a boat, even something seemingly as simple as "Is there an airport nearby where a plane large enough to carry a digital VTR can land?" affect what equipment can be used. Believe it or not, the answer to that last question is not always yes—even in the U.S. You can find yourself (as REBO crews have) in the position of being forced to drive hundreds of miles farther than you want to.

Figure 3.2—Loading gear in a small plane in Kenya

Experience has shown that it is a good idea to pack High Definition video equipment for shipment in bulky (though not necessarily heavy) packages that are too big to be easily hand carried by one person.

Figure 3.3—Waiting with the gear at an airport in Vietnam

Equipment packed this way has a tendency to arrive in better condition at the other end, because it can't just be picked up and tossed carelessly around.

Experience has also shown that applying "shockwatches" to the exterior of cases that contain delicate equipment is a good idea. Shockwatches are devices that measure G-force acceleration and indicate when a package has been dropped or otherwise abused. Use of these devices tells shippers (and insurers) you are serious about the proper care of your gear.

Tape Stock

Not only is the cost of HD tape stock an issue (a one-hour reel of 1" digital tape stock costs three to four times what one hour of UNIHI stock costs, and UNIHI stock costs about five times what BetaSP does), but there are also durability, weight, and interchange compatibility issues to consider. The cost of tape stock has an effect on the total amount of shooting that can be cost effective. To improve the shooting ratio, more careful shot planning is required in High Definition video than for standard definition video.

It is common practice to make protection dubs for every camera and edit master, to guard against the failure or loss of a master tape. The tape costs required to make these protections must also be factored into the budget.

Length	1" HDD	UNIHI	W-VHS	D1	BetaSP
Three hours	n/a	n/a	$85	n/a	n/a
Two hours	n/a	n/a	$65	n/a	n/a
One hour	$1200	$310	n/a (in US)	$330	$80
30 minutes	$700	$n/a	n/a (in US)	$190	$60

Table 3.1—Approximate tape stock costs

Using the figures in Table 3.1, a BetaSP job that used three, one-hour camera masters and one, 30-minute edit master on D1 would jump from a tape budget of about $425 for camera and edit masters, to about $1000 when figuring in protection dubs and adding in some contingency for music and B-roll. A comparable High Definition production using UNIHI tape jumps from about $1600 to about $3500, assuming the camera protection dubs were made on UNIHI tape (which is not the best way to do it—1" digital is the best way, adding another $4300 to the tape budget). That same production using 1" digital HD stock would jump from about $4000 to almost $9000. Each additional 1" reel of High Definition camera or edit master stock has a significant impact on the final tape budget.

Weight

A one hour 1" reel of digital tape stock contains three times the amount of tape of a 1" Type-C reel, making it much heavier, which also increases shipping costs. This additional weight usually does not have an impact on portability. If you will be using a 1" VTR you're either in a studio or you have some vehicle rigged up to act as an engineering truck.

Tape Interchange Compatibility

While UNIHI cassette tapes are less expensive, more compact, and more robust than their open reel counterparts, there have been compatibility problems when trying, for example, to play tapes that have been recorded on a Sony (studio) UNIHI machine on Panasonic (studio) UNIHI machines. The problems have usually revealed themselves as visible head switching glitches. This incompatibility may be a relatively isolated occurrence that may have to do simply with the number of machines manufactured to date, but it may affect postproduction, if there is a compatibility problem between the record VTR and the edit VTRs.

Audio Production

There are absolutely no technical differences between recording audio for High Definition video and recording audio for standard definition video or film.

Figure 3.4—Field audio recording in Vietnam

Double system audio can be used, where audio is recorded on an external audio recorder (usually a DAT machine with timecode capability). In these cases any audio recorded on the VTR is usually only for reference purposes.

Figure 3.5—Field audio recording in France

The multitrack audio recording capabilities of most HD VTRs, shown in Table 3.2, open up new and interesting creative possibilities in the field and in the studio. The multitrack audio capabilities also raise some interesting audio distribution possibilities. For example, the Sony HDD–1000's eight audio channels are capable of handling up to four separate stereo programs, making possible the simultaneous distribution of multilingual programming on the same piece of tape.

VTR	Tape Format(s)	# of Channels Audio Formats
Sony HDD–1000	1" open reel	8 PCM
Sony HDV–10	UNIHI cassette	4 PCM
Panasonic AU–1500 (studio)	UNIHI cassette	4 PCM
Panasonic AU–1400 (portable)	UNIHI cassette	2 PCM
JVC SR–W320U	W-VHS cassette VHS/S-VHS cassette	Stereo Hi-Fi Monaural

Table 3.2—VTR multitrack audio capabilities

Environmental Issues

Because of the high data rates involved, High Definition VTRs have a tendency to be much more susceptible to problems caused by humidity, dust, and dirt than their traditional video counterparts. 1" digital High Definition VTRs are especially susceptible to adverse environmental conditions. On any productions using these VTRs, an air conditioned, clean, relatively low humidity environment should be provided.

While studio UNIHI VTRs are more forgiving of environmental conditions they are not as forgiving as BetaSP VTRs. However, they are getting better. Air conditioning is no longer critical to the success of UNIHI production using a studio deck, but care should be taken in very hot locations, especially to keep the VTR out of direct sunlight.

Notwithstanding these general care guidelines, in over two years of shooting with the Panasonic portable UNIHI VTR, REBO engineers have encountered only two problems in the field, both of which they were alerted to by the VTR. One of these was when the deck was being used in an incredibly hot and humid environment. REBO engineers have *never* had a record problem go unnoticed in the field.

As in all video productions, tape should be kept cool and out of direct sunlight. This is especially true for 1" digital tapes, which have been known to shed their oxide coating with very little environmental provocation.

Finally, standard precautions should be taken when moving video equipment in and out of hot and humid environments and cool environments.

Studio Versus Location Production

There are no significant differences between shooting High Definition video in a studio and shooting either film or standard definition in a studio. However, the high noise level of the Sony HDD–1000 1" digital VTR or one of the studio UNIHI VTRs may require that some kind of sound barrier be erected, or that the VTR and camera control area be moved away from the set or be placed in a camera truck.

Live Multicamera Production

For a discussion of many of the issues involved in live multicamera production, refer to *Woodstock '94: Live Multicamera Production Integrating High Definition Video and NTSC* beginning on page 100.

Integrating High Definition and NTSC Video and Audio

For a discussion of many of the issues involved in integrating High Definition and NTSC video and audio refer to *Woodstock '94: Live Multicamera Production Integrating High Definition Video and NTSC* beginning on page 100 and *High Definition/Standard Definition Compatibility Issues* beginning on page 62.

Choosing a Production Package

In addition to the shoot logistics—the locations and the types of shots that are needed—the final release format and postproduction considerations also have an influence on the choice of the production package. These issues also need to be considered in film and standard definition video productions, but the choices and trade-offs are not as well understood when shooting High Definition video.

During preproduction, it helps to ask the following questions focusing specifically on the following issues to help select the right equipment:

1 What is the primary use for the footage? What, if any, are the secondary uses for the footage?

For example, what postproduction effects will be used? Is it a straightforward editing job, or are there lots of special effects involved? Is the footage being produced specifically for integration with, and release on, film?

2 How portable and mobile do you need to be?

Will you be shooting in the studio, or primarily on location? Where are the locations? Can you drive a truck to them? How close can you get the truck? Are there any shots that require the camera operator to be especially mobile, perhaps using a Steadicam rig?

3 Are there any other special requirements?

For example, is an unusual lens required to get a specific shot?

Selecting the Right Equipment for the Job

Camera Options

At present, the Sony HDC–500 camera provides the highest quality images of any High Definition video camera. Some say that it might be the best camera in the world, bar none.

In general, CCD cameras are preferred over Saticon tube cameras (the Sony HDC–300) for sensitivity, stability, and ease of setup and use. However, there are any number of reasons why a production may use an HDC—300 camera and produce quality results. Table 3.3 compares target size, sensor type, sensor resolution, and sensitivity/speed of all currently available High Definition video cameras.

Camera	Sensor Size/Type Resolution	Sensitivity/ Speed
Sony HDC–300	3, 1" Tube Full bandwidth	~64 ASA
Sony HDC–500	3, 1" CCD 1.987 million pixels	~F8@2000 lux
Panasonic AK–HC900	4, 2/3"CCD 1.3 million pixels	~f4@2000 lux ~100–125 ASA
JVC KH–100U	3, 2/3" CCD 1.0 million pixels	~f7@2000 lux ~250–320 ASA

Table 3.3—Camera sensor, target size, resolution, and speed

It is worth noting that sensitivity/speed ratings will vary depending on the measurer and other conditions. For example, the Sony HDC–500 is rated by Sony at 500 ASA, but some DPs prefer to rate it at 320, because they feel that that rating gives them better separation in the blacks. Refer to *Neil Smith* beginning on page 132 for more discussion on this point.

Table 3.4 compares maximum horizontal resolution in pixels of all currently available High Definition video cameras.

Camera	Maximum Horizontal Resolution
Sony HDC–300	1920 pixels
Sony HDC–500	1920 pixels
Panasonic AK–HC900	1440 pixels
JVC KH–100U	960 pixels

Table 3.4—Camera resolution

Lens Options

The relatively small number of High Definition video cameras available means that there is a correspondingly small assortment of High Definition-specific lenses to choose from. This relatively small lens selection has an affect on shot selection, which in turn has an effect on creative direction and production design. Table 3.5 on page 39 shows the relative availability of lenses for High Definition cameras.

The Panavision-modified Sony HDC–300 camera is only superior to other studio High Definition video cameras in that it accepts the full complement of Panavision lenses and accessories. Panavision lenses and accessories have not yet been adapted to the Sony HDC–500 camera.

Both the Panasonic AK–HC900 and JVC KH–100U cameras have a Sony-type Betacam lens mount, making it possible to use a host of NTSC lenses. Only a small number of High Definition-specific lenses with Sony-type Betacam mounts have been designed, and their use is recommended wherever possible.

Furthermore, NTSC lenses designated for EFP use are preferred over those designated for ENG use.

Camera	Lens Mount	Comparative Lens Selection
Sony HDC–300	Custom	Low
Panavision/Sony HDC–300	Panavision	High (not the entire complement of Panavision lenses)
Sony HDC–500	Custom	Low
Panasonic AK–HC900	Sony type Betacam	Medium (HD–specific) High (EFP Betacam)
JVC KH–100U	Sony type Betacam	Medium (HD–specific) High (EFP Betacam)

Table 3.5—Comparative lens selection

Table 3.6 compares the horizontal angle of view and focal length (in mm) of lenses for High Definition video cameras with 1" and 2/3" targets, lenses for 4:3 standard definition video, lenses for 16mm and 35mm film cameras, and lenses for 35mm still cameras.

The view angles and focal lengths were generated using standard formulae, which can be found in the American Society of Cinematographers' *American Cinematographer Manual.* Many values have been rounded up or down, so the values should be considered to be approximate only.

In practice, it is wise to choose a lens that is slightly wider at the wide end and slightly tighter at the long end to provide some additional flexibility in camera positioning.

Cinematographers can feel comfortable equating the High Definition 1" target with Super16 to get an approximate feel for lens equivalence.

VTR Options

The Sony HDD–1000 digital 1" open reel VTR records and reproduces the highest quality images of any VTR in the world. But that quality comes at the price of portability as well as in the high cost of tape stock (refer back to Table 3.1 on page 35).

Horizontal View Angle	Focal Length (mm)					
	1" target 16:9	2/3" target 16:9	2/3" target 4:3	35mm still 3:2	35mm motion	16mm motion
80°	8	6	5.5	21	13	6
50°	15	10	9	39	24	11
40°	19	13	12	50	30	14
30°	26	18	16.5	67	41	19
20°	40	28	26	105	63	30
15°	52	36	33	135	82	38
10°	79	55	50	205	125	58
7.5°	105	73	67	270	165	78
5°	160	110	101	415	252	118

Table 3.6—Comparative lens focal lengths

The UNIHI cassette format is much more portable than 1" digital tape, and is suitable for a very broad range of High Definition video applications as a camera master, edit source master in an interformat edit suite, and distribution format.

For editing purposes, the 1" digital VTR is recommended in *all* instances, especially for multigeneration effects work.

Table 3.7 compares the tape format, recording format, and audio recording capabilities of currently available High Definition VTRs.

VTR	Tape Format Recording Format	# of Channels Audio Format
Sony HDD–1000	1" open reel YPbPr Component Digital	8 PCM
Sony HDV–10	UNIHI cassette YPbPr Component Analog	4 PCM
Panasonic AU–1500 (studio)	UNIHI cassette YPbPr Component Analog	4 PCM
Panasonic AU–1400 (portable)	UNIHI cassette YPbPr Component Analog	2 PCM
JVC SR–W320U	W-VHS cassette YPbPr Component Analog VHS/S-VHS NTSC/S-video	Stereo Hi-Fi Mono/Stereo

Table 3.7—VTR tape format, recording format, and audio capabilities

Few High Definition video VTRs accept microphone level inputs directly, requiring that an outboard mixer be used. All VTRs have direct audio monitoring capabilities via headphone.

Equipment Power Requirements

Refer to *Power* beginning on page 53 for more information on powering equipment.

Quickie Camera/VTR Package Selection Guide

The recommendations here are just that, recommendations. Like many 'rules,' the recommendations are just guidelines and not hard and fast 'musts,' and in many cases very good results can be achieved using alternate packages. However, they are based on more than ten years of production experience in High Definition video in lots of different situations.

For Transfer to Film

The primary consideration when shooting High Definition video for film is to obtain the highest quality images possible. For these reasons, the Sony HDC–500 camera and the Sony HDD–1000 1" digital VTR is the recommended package.

For Special Effects

As when shooting High Definition video for film, the objective is to obtain the highest quality images possible. Again, the Sony HDC–500 camera and the Sony HDD–1000 1" digital VTR is the recommended package.

The reason to take an Ultimatte into a shooting situation is be able to gauge the quality of the lighting of the blue or green screen, the quality of the mattes generated, and to match blue/green screen elements and the other layers of the composite *as the individual elements are being shot.*

This is especially valuable when there are complex interactions between layers; it is possible for the director and DP to see the interaction as the take goes down to get the best possible effect.

For more on lighting for blue/green screen work, see *John Alonzo* beginning on page 109 and *Neil Smith* beginning on page 132.

For Broadcast and Documentaries

When getting the highest possible quality images is important, portability is not really an issue (for example, you're in a studio or you can work from a truck), and cost is an issue, opt for the Sony HDC–500 camera and a studio UNIHI VTR, either the Sony HDV–10 or the Panasonic AU–HD1500.

When getting the highest possible quality images is important, but so is portability, opt for the Sony HDC–500 camera and the Panasonic AU–HD1400 portable UNIHI VTR.

When portability, mobility, and flexibility in lens selection is important, opt for the Panasonic AK–HC900 camera and the Panasonic AU–HD1400 portable UNIHI VTR.

Other Package Considerations

Sony's fiber-optic system, which can be used only with the HDC–300 and HDC–500 cameras, makes it possible to get the camera as far away as 1000 meters from the CCU.

The Sony HDC–500 is more sensitive than either the Panasonic AK–HC900 or JVC KH–100U. Consider using the 500 when you know you are going to be shooting in very low light situations.

Camera/VTR Packages in Depth

Package 1...Very High Quality, Not Very Portable

This package consists of either the Sony HDC–500 or the Sony HDC–300 camera and the Sony HDD–1000 1" digital VTR. Wherever possible, opt for the CCD-based HDC–500; it is smaller, lighter, and several stops more sensitive than the HDC–300.

To monitor video quality, an 18" High Definition video monitor is included in this package. While smaller High Definition video monitors are available, the 18" monitor is the smallest monitor that is recommended for serious quality monitoring. Smaller monitors cannot hope to display all of the information in the picture, and it is possible to miss subtle problems. In fact, some engineers insist on using a 28" monitor, claiming (correctly) that even the 18" monitor is incapable of showing very subtle noise problems. Experience has shown, however, that most problems are viewable on an 18" monitor.

It is the VTR and monitor that reduce the portability of this package. Very much at home in a studio, this package requires a substantial truck or equivalent environment, with both types of AC—alternating current and air conditioning—if it is going to be used in the field.

Figure 3.6 displays the configuration used for *Fool's Fire* (see page 89) and *The Astronomer's Dream* (see page 92).

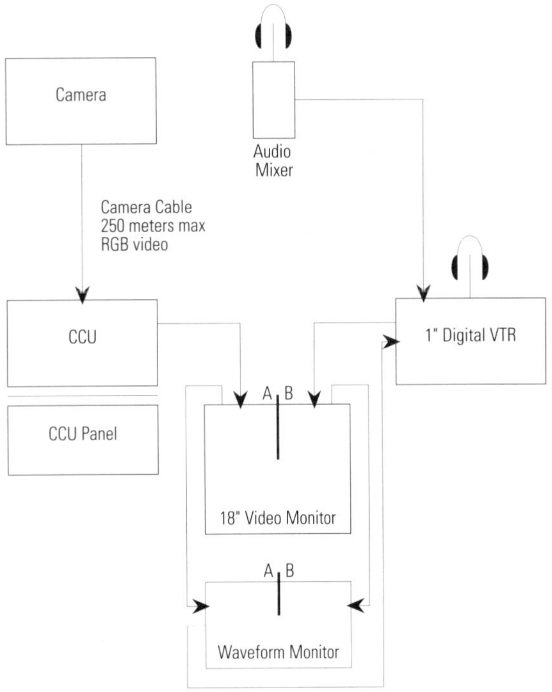

Figure 3.6—Package 1, Very High Quality, Not Very Portable

Figure 3.6 shows how the package would be cabled for a single-camera production. The configuration also includes a method for cabling in a waveform monitor for monitoring video quality.

Package 2...Transportable

This package consists of either the Sony HDC–500 or the Panasonic AK–HC900 camera and a studio UNIHI VTR, either the Sony HDV–10 or the Panasonic AU–HD1500.

These configurations are used when it is necessary to be somewhat mobile, but at the same time, it is important to monitor video quality and record a high quality signal. The studio UNIHI VTRs have playback capability (the Panasonic portable UNIHI is record-only), which enable confidence playback of tapes in the field.

Figure 3.7—Why it's called "transportable"

This package fits comfortably into a cargo van which has all of the rear seats removed and the windows blacked out, and it can be powered by a gas-powered generator or an inverter tied into the engineering vehicle's battery—just make sure you've got enough gas to keep the engine running. (See Figure 4.3 on page 54 for an illustration showing one way to power equipment and to keep all your batteries charged.)

Once again, an 18" High Definition video monitor is included in this package to monitor video quality. As mentioned previously, smaller High Definition video monitors are available, but the 18" monitor is the smallest monitor that is recommended for serious quality monitoring. Smaller monitors cannot hope to display all of the information in the picture, and it is possible to miss subtle problems.

This package is also suitable for on location EFP-style work where mobility is not important once the engineering position (VTR and camera control) is set.

Figure 3.8 displays a simplified configuration showing how the package would be cabled for a single-camera production. The configuration also includes a method for cabling in a waveform monitor for an additional video quality monitoring step.

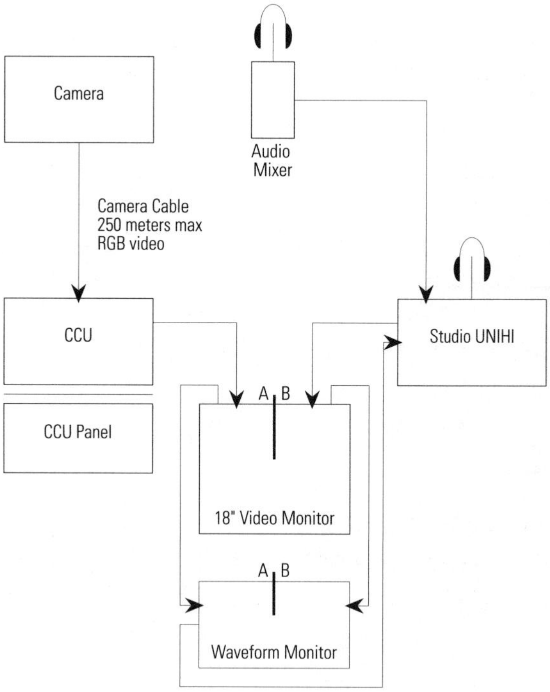

Figure 3.8—Package 2, Transportable

Package 3...Portable #1

This package consists of either the Sony HDC–500, or the Panasonic AK–HC900 camera, and the Panasonic AU–HD1400 portable UNIHI VTR.

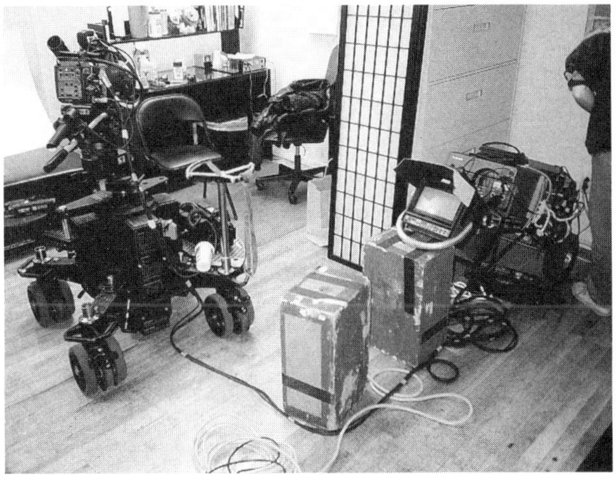

Figure 3.9—Portable rig with 9" HD monitor

The package gets used when it is necessary to be very mobile, and at the same time, to provide some reasonable level of video monitoring—a small, usually 9", High Definition video monitor but no waveform monitor. The engineer needs to pay very careful attention to what is going on, because there is no objective measure of the quality of the video signal without the waveform monitor; noise and RF will be very difficult to see. Also, immediate confidence playback of video is not available because the VTR is record-only.

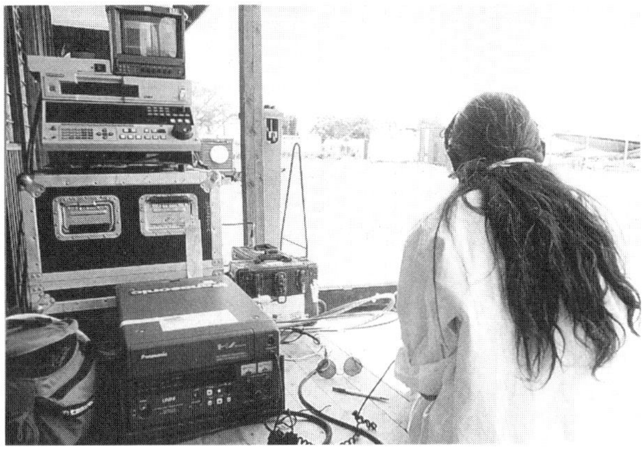

Figure 3.10—Using a studio UNIHI for confidence playback in Kenya

This package fits comfortably onto a small handtruck and can be powered entirely by batteries.

Figure 3.9 displays the configuration used for *New York: On The Edge,* (see page 98).

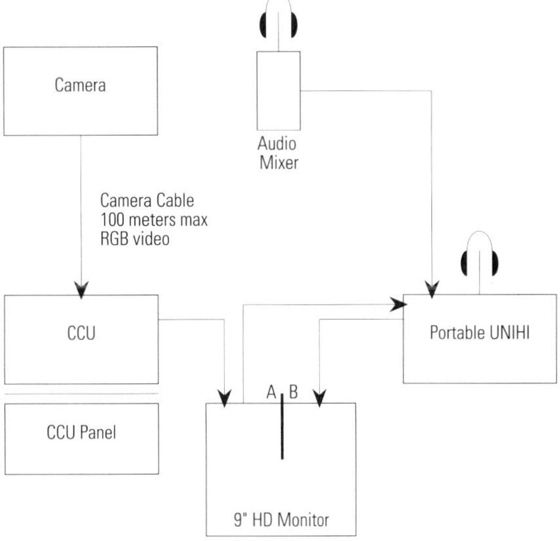

Figure 3.11—Package 3, Portable #1

Figure 3.11 shows how the package is cabled for a single-camera production. If a battery-powered downconverter is being used to provide an NTSC video feed, the downconverter can receive its input looped out of the 9" monitor

Package 4...Portable #2

This package consists of either the Sony HDC–500, or the Panasonic AK–HC900 camera, and the Panasonic AU–HD1400 portable UNIHI VTR.

The package is used when it is necessary to be very mobile and to have some ability to monitor the video. The monitoring capability is provided by a battery-operated High Definition to NTSC downconverter and a small, usually 9", NTSC monitor, though a 4" NTSC monitor is often used.

When shooting in this configuration, the monitoring ability does not provide any opportunity for real quality control. For example, the engineer can't see RF or other noise in the monitor unless it is exceptionally bad, nor is it possible to make color balance judgments. The engineer can help with decisions about iris and framing, and can tell if the camera balances when the white and black balance controls are used.

Figure 3.12—Monitoring video on a 4" NTSC monitor on a hillside in Uganda

This package fits comfortably onto a small handtruck and can be powered entirely by batteries. Confidence playback of video is not available because the VTR is record-only.

Figure 3.13—Engineering on a river in Vietnam

Figure 3.14 displays a simplified configuration showing how the package can be cabled.

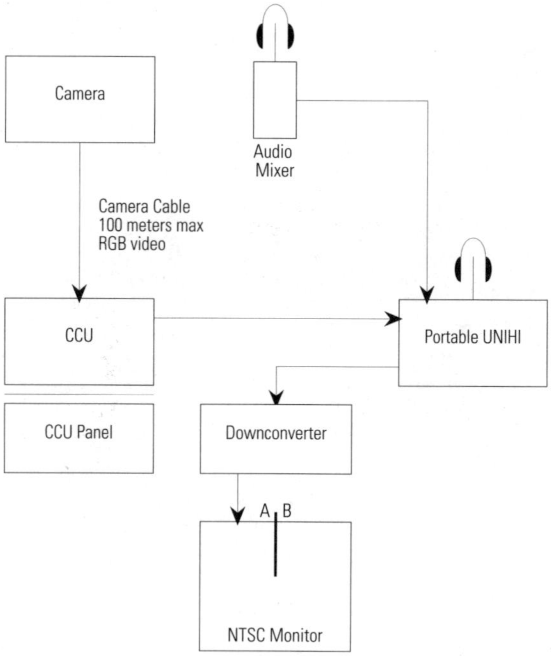

Figure 3.14—Package 4, Portable #2

Package 5...Very Portable

The most portable configuration consists of just the Panasonic AK–HC900 camera connected directly to the record-only Panasonic AU–HD1400 UNIHI VTR by a standard VTR cable.

Although VTR cables can be up to fifteen meters in length before roll-off becomes visible, cable lengths of not more than ten meters are recommended. Because the camera is cabled directly to the VTR, the camera must be set to output YPbPr.

In this configuration, the lack of a CCU and video monitor for engineering means that greater care needs to be taken in the field to produce technically usable material.

The camera person needs to be capable of gauging image quality through the viewfinder, but, as is the case with virtually every viewfinder made, it will be impossible to catch everything through the viewfinder.

Figure 3.15—Using the very portable rig in a jeep, part 1

Special care must be taken to make sure that lenses and filters are perfectly clean before each shot. A piece of lint from a cleaning cloth left on a filter can render a critical shot useless, because the piece of lint may not be visible in the viewfinder.

Figure 3.16—Using the very portable rig in a jeep, part 2

This package is used only when portability and mobility are the prime factors, for example, it can be used in moving vehicles.

Figure 3.17 displays a simplified configuration showing how the package is cabled.

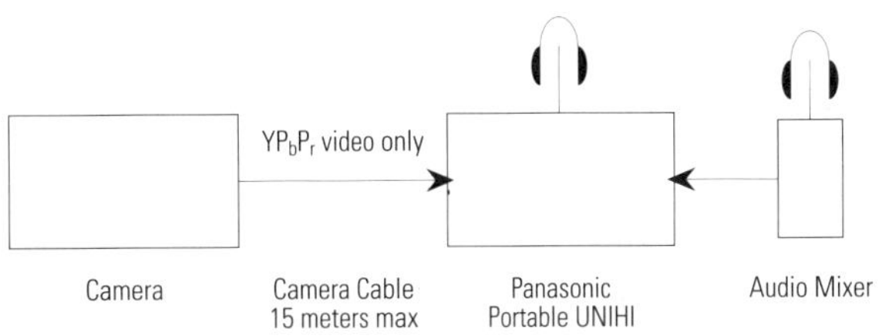

Figure 3.17—Package 5, Very Portable

Wacky Camera/VTR Packages

Some camera/VTR packages just don't make sense, because they are based on a mismatch between the capabilities of the camera and the VTR. It is possible to shoot this way, but it's either financial or technical overkill.

Wacky Package Idea #1

In Wacky Package #1, the camera does not live up to the capabilities of the VTR. The worst example of this would be to use the JVC–KH100U camera with the Sony HDD–1000 VTR. The VTR is capable of recording a full-bandwidth signal, but the camera can only output a half-bandwidth signal. Shooting with this package is a waste of very expensive tape.

The next worst example would be to use the Panasonic AK–HC900 camera and the HDD–1000 VTR. The AK–HC900 was designed specifically to be used with a UNIHI VTR and outputs a two-thirds bandwidth signal.

Wacky Package Idea #2

In Wacky Package Idea #2, the VTR does not live up to the capabilities of the camera.

The worst examples of this would be to use either the Sony HDC–500 or HDC–300 camera with the JVC SR–320U W-VHS VTR. Both of the cameras output a full resolution image, but the VTR records less than half the luminance bandwidth and only one-fifth the luminance bandwidth of a Sony HDD–1000 VTR.

Interesting Uses for VTRs

Does your production need dailies for offline screening? Consider using the JVC SR–W320U to record dailies in parallel. It's cheap, fast, and convenient, and because there is no separate NTSC downconversion step, the recording keeps more of the detail of the original image.

The JVC SR–W320U is also a good VTR to consider installing in a corporate boardroom or similar screening environment. W-VHS tapes are inexpensive when compared with UNIHI and 1" tapes, and a single W-VHS tape can hold up to three hours of High Definition video or up to nine hours of S-VHS video.

Special Rigs

See *Jib Arms, Dollies, Cranes, Motion Control Systems, and Steadicam* on page 57.

Chapter 4

Engineering

In High Definition video, good engineering is pivotal to the success of a project. High Definition video engineers are more than mere technicians; they play a central role in the conception and execution of the project working in close partnership with the producer, the director, the DP, the camera operator(s), the grips, utilities, and electrics.

REBO has been very lucky not only to have very talented and dedicated engineers, but to have two such engineers who have been with the company for more than a decade. This continuity, in conjunction with a creative urge and the necessary technical skills to design and build equipment to solve specific problems, accounts, in no small measure, for the success that REBO has enjoyed in pulling off productions that regularly challenge the limits of what it has been possible to achieve in High Definition video. Getting their experiences down on paper, so that others can take advantage of their knowledge and insights into the craft of engineering High Definition video, is one of the primary reasons for writing this book.

This chapter will not only cover High Definition video production issues from an engineering viewpoint, it will also disclose some very important facts that, for some reason, the manuals never seem to tell you.

Things to Keep in Mind

1 High Definition video is more sensitive to timing differences than standard definition video.

For this reason, more than usual care must be taken to ensure that the total lengths of all cables match closely.

2 Most High Definition video gear has both GBR and YPbPr inputs and outputs.

It is important, therefore, to make sure that wiring is consistent: GBR to GBR or YPbPr to YPbPr. Monitors usually have GBR/YPbPr switches, so it's not always easy to tell with a glance if the wiring in the system is consistent. Getting **color spaces** swapped can result in an expensive reshoot or reedit. Check. Check again.

3 Always take monitoring and diagnostic equipment and a repair tool kit on every shoot.

4 Whenever you digitize something, always try to record a linear ramp. Missing bits or other inaccuracies in an A/D to D/A conversion step can be seen as uneven steps in the image.

5 Unless there is no other choice, avoid trying to color correct in YPbPr color space. It is very difficult.

6 When possible, take a two-frame framestore (like the REBO Research ReStore™) on location to grab digital stills for continuity. The framestore can cut between two images or between a still image and live video, making highly accurate comparisons of lighting, color correction, and propping fast and easy.

7 When dedicated playback confidence equipment is not available, a portable High Definition video to NTSC downconverter can be used for monitoring. While this is not a preferred (or even recommended) method for assessing quality, it at least gives you some idea of what's going on when other alternatives are not available.

8 When shooting sequences for special effects use, try to have an Ultimatte (or other compositing device) on the set with you to check the quality of the mattes as you shoot.

The Expanded Role of the Engineer

As was mentioned in the introduction to this chapter, good engineering is pivotal to the success of a High Definition video project. During production, the engineer is responsible for maintaining good communication with the director, the DP, and the camera operator(s). One of the main reasons for this is that, at the moment, there is no High Definition video camcorder. The engineer must start and stop the tape manually and must call out when the VTR is up to speed. The engineer must also be watching the video monitor closely, looking for technical defects in the picture—including checking for focus in low-light shooting situations (the viewfinders in the cameras are not really up to the task of really precise focus), and communicating what they see to the director, DP, camera operator, or other members of the crew.

For more on the importance of communication, see *John Alonzo* beginning on page 109.

What does it take to become a proficient High Definition video engineer? A lot of patience, for one thing. Paying attention to details, for another. The ability to communicate well. A passion for wanting to get the best image possible also helps a lot, as does a strong urge to get involved in many creative aspects of a project as well as solving the strictly technical problems.

Oh. A lot of practice helps. While the basics of engineering High Definition video are in the main very similar to the basics of engineering standard definition video, familiarity with the equipment and the ability to troubleshoot under pressure can only come through regular use. We can tell you all we know about the craft of engineering High Definition video, but there is no substitute for actual experience.

The working relationships between the engineer and the producer, director, and DP, are discussed in *John Alonzo* beginning on page 109, *Charles R. Caillouet, Jr.* beginning on page 114, and *Philip Hack* beginning on page 122.

Cameras

High Definition video CCD cameras are, thankfully, more sensitive than the earlier tube cameras; before their introduction, available light in High Definition video was synonymous with bright sunny days.

Camera	Sensor Size/Type Resolution	Sensitivity/ Speed
Sony HDC–300	3, 1" Tube Full bandwidth	~64 ASA
Sony HDC–500	3, 1" CCD 1.987 million pixels	~F8@2000 lux ~500–600 ASA*
Panasonic AK–HC900	4, 2/3"CCD 1.3 million pixels	~f4@2000 lux ~100–125 ASA
JVC KH–100U	3, 2/3" CCD 1.0 million pixels	~f7@2000 lux ~250–320 ASA
Note: Some DPs contend that the HDC–500 should be rated at 320 ASA.		

Table 4.1—Camera target size, sensor type, resolution, and speed

CCD cameras deliver higher S/N (signal-to-noise) ratios than tube cameras, resulting in cleaner looking pictures. CCD cameras also have extended dynamic range when compared with tube cameras, however the recordable dynamic range still falls short of film.

CCD cameras are more prone to **aliasing** than tube cameras. While not visible in most situations, certain kinds of high-frequency source material are very good at showing up the aliasing tendencies of CCD-based cameras.

It should be noted that High Definition tube cameras are considered obsolete. At least there aren't any models in production. But this does not mean that you should not consider using an HDC–300 camera, if the situation calls for it: you may not have a choice. At the moment, to pull off a large multicamera shoot in North America will almost certainly require a mix of cameras, including HDC–300s. It is important to keep in mind that using an HDC–300 may have an impact on lighting requirements; unless you are shooting outdoors on a bright sunny day, you will probably need more. Also, you will have to schedule more time for camera maintenance when using an HDC–300. Among other things, tubes drift and need registering.

For more on mixing cameras in live multicamera productions see *Woodstock '94: Live Multicamera Production Integrating High Definition Video and NTSC* beginning on page 100 and *Philip Hack* beginning on page 122.

Sony HDC–500

There are a number of camera control (CCU and operations panel) configurations. One for studio operations, or where the engineering position is fixed, and two others for various degrees of portability and control.

The studio camera control configuration consists of a camera signal processor and a camera control panel. This configuration provides the engineer with the greatest level of control over the various settings of the camera. However, a special camera cable must be used.

For portable production, the camera can be used with or without a box called a signal distributor. The signal distributor allows the use of longer cables (100 meters, as opposed to 25 meters without it) as well as the use of a standard VTR cable from the signal distributor to the VTR. The signal distributor can be run off DC or AC.

There are two remote control panels, one of which can be handheld very easily. They vary in the number of controls they offer engineers. Both of these panels can be plugged directly into the camera or into the signal distributor, and can be located up to 25 meters away.

Panasonic AK–HC900

The Panasonic camera will accept any NTSC-type video lens that has a Sony-type Betacam mount. REBO's standby lens for this camera is a Fujinon HA12x8.5ERD–R28, which is a 2/3" High Definition-specific lens.

The portable UNIHI VTR has only YPbPr video inputs. When the camera is connected directly to the portable VTR, it is necessary to switch the camera output to YPbPr. However, when using the remote operations panels and CCU, the camera must be set for GBR output with the CCU performing the conversion between GBR and YPbPr. The GBR/YPbPr switch is inside the camera itself, and it is good practice to check the setting of the switch.

There is E-to-E monitoring on the output of the VTR, so if there is an engineering monitor (which is not always the case when shooting with the camera connected directly to the VTR), the setting of the switch can be checked that way.

When the camera is connected directly to the VTR, shutter speed adjustments are limited. The CCU provides much more flexibility.

Lenses

CCD cameras can't correct for chromatic aberrations in lenses, and individual colors can't be back focused (as they can be in tube cameras). The lack of electronic and mechanical adjustments means that CCD cameras require higher quality lenses because many potential lens problems that can be compensated for in a tube camera simply can't be fixed in a CCD camera.

Commonly available NTSC lenses do not usually meet the resolution requirements of High Definition video, and should be selected with care. When unsure of the suitability of a particular lens, it is best to make an assessment by trying out the specific lens.

When using a High Definition video camera with a Sony-type Betacam mount—which means that standard definition video lenses can be used—choose lenses that are designated 'EFP' (electronic field production) over those that are designated 'ENG' (electronic news gathering). In general, EFP lenses are higher quality than ENG lenses. Fujinon makes a line of Sony-type Betacam-mount lenses which are specifically designated as HD lenses.

To accommodate the transition between 4:3 and 16:9 format video, some manufacturers have created lenses that can be switched between the two aspect ratios. One of the results of switching the aspect ratio this way is that the focal length of the lens changes, as can be seen in Table 4.2.

Horizontal View Angle	Focal Length (mm)	
	2/3" target, 16:9	2/3" target, 4:3
80°	6	5.5
50°	10	9
40°	13	12
30°	18	16.5
20°	28	26
15°	36	33
10°	55	50
7.5°	73	67
5°	110	101

Table 4.2—Focal length difference in 4:3 and 16:9 lenses

Table 3.6 on page 39, shows a more complete comparison of horizontal viewing angles and focal lengths for a variety of aspect ratios and target sizes.

Using Lens Accessories

Because the quality of High Definition video encourages the use of filters and other accessories (see *Neil Smith* beginning on page 132), it is important to look for vignetting when a matte box is being used.

VTRs

At present, there are three different High Definition videotape formats; 1" digital (open reel), UNIHI (cassette), and W-VHS (cassette). Table 4.3 shows common High Definition and standard definition VTR formats.

	Digital/ Analog	**Component/ Composite**
1" HDD	Digital	Component
UNIHI	Analog	Component
W-VHS	Analog	Component
D1	Digital	Component
D2	Digital	Composite
BetaSP	Analog	Composite

Table 4.3—VTR formats

1" digital tape is used solely by the Sony HDD–1000 VTR. The tape transport is the size of a 1" Type-C VTR, and there is a separate digital processing unit. Together, the transport and processor unit weigh approximately 575 pounds in shipping cases, which makes them unsuitable for productions where portability and mobility are an issue.

The HDD–1000 and the tape stock are sensitive to environmental conditions, so it is wise to operate them only in climate controlled conditions. Furthermore, it is not feasible to power the HDD–1000 from a DC source through an inverter. AC power is required, either from a mains source or from a substantial generator.

There are a number of VTRs from a variety of manufacturers that use the UNIHI tape format. Sony and Panasonic both make studio versions of the UNIHI (HDV–10 and AU–HD1500, respectively) that, at 175 pounds in a traveling case, could be called 'transportable.' These two studio UNIHIs can be operated off AC as well as off a DC source through an inverter (see *Inverters* on page 54). Panasonic also makes a portable UNIHI VTR (see *Panasonic AU–HD1400 Portable UNIHI* on page 53).

JVC has introduced a format called W-VHS. The W-VHS format is lower in quality than UNIHI, but the VTR has the ability to record up to three hours on a surprisingly inexpensive cassette. The deck also has the ability to record and play back standard VHS as well as S-VHS cassettes. We at REBO have virtually no experience using the VTR because most clients have indicated that they are unwilling to accept programs that have been produced in this format.

From a production standpoint, it looks like the VTR is a consumer unit and may not be up to the rigors of demanding field production.

Table 4.4 shows the recording bandwidths of each of the VTRs and tape formats.

VTR	**Record Bandwidth Y, Pb, Pr in MHz**
Sony HDD–1000 (1" open reel)	30, 15, 15
Sony HDV–10 (UNIHI)	20, 7, 7
Panasonic AU–1500 (UNIHI)	20, 7, 7
Panasonic AU–1400 (UNIHI)	20, 7, 7
JVC SR–W320U (W–VHS)	13.3, 4, 4

Table 4.4—Recording bandwidths of each of the VTRs and tape formats

Table 4.5 shows video inputs and outputs for each VTR.

VTR	Video Input(s), Output(s) Connectors
Sony HDD–1000	RGB, YPbPr BNC
Sony HDV–10	RGB, YPbPr BNC
Panasonic AU–1500 (studio)	RGB, YPbPr BNC
Panasonic AU–1400 (portable)	YPbPr BNC, 26-pin VTR cable
JVC SR–W320U	YPbPr RCA

Table 4.5—VTR video inputs and outputs

Panasonic AU–HD1400 Portable UNIHI

The portable (55 pound) UNIHI VTR is a "record-only" VTR. Another way of saying this, is that it is a "no-playback" VTR. It has only YPbPr video inputs and outputs. It can record two channels of digital audio and has only XLR connectors, which are the reverse gender from what is considered normal in the United States. The VTR can be powered by 12 volt batteries or by AC using the appropriate power supply. REBO engineers have always powered the VTR on batteries even when AC is available.

The manual recommends that the VTR be used to record only when it is in a horizontal position. Experience shows that tapes recorded when the VTR is in a vertical position are just fine, except for the beginning three to four minutes of tape. Furthermore, problems ejecting tapes when the VTR is vertical have been reported. As a general rule, try to keep the VTR as nearly horizontal as practical and comfortable for the engineer. REBO engineers tend to work with the VTR at 45 degrees, with the front of the VTR and the engineering monitor facing up, as can be seen in Figure 4.1.

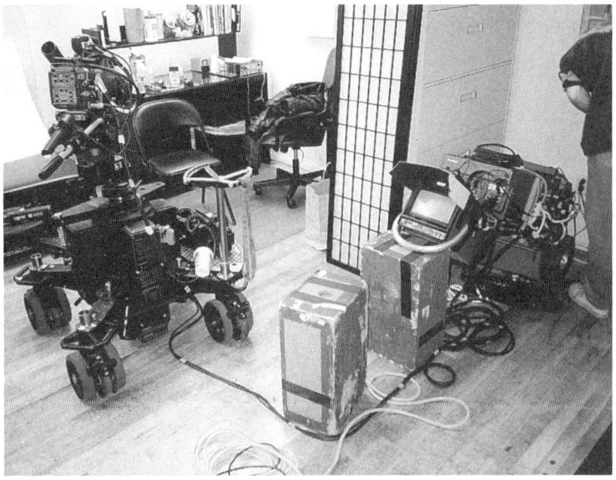

Figure 4.1—Orienting the AU–HD1400 VTR

Power

One key to successfully shooting on location with any type of video gear is making sure that everything gets powered properly. With High Definition video this is especially true because everything requires more power.

Powering Cameras

Even when it is possible to power the camera head down the camera cable, use separate batteries at the camera head to prolong overall battery life. There is a lot of power wasted in the electrical resistance of the cable when it is being powered from the CCU. Only power the camera down the cable if running out of power is not an issue.

Generators

High Definition video imposes no special requirements on generators, except perhaps, that you might need to get a bigger one than you would for an NTSC shoot. Look for a generator that is well regulated and is as quiet as possible.

Using the techniques that are described for using inverters and batteries, you may find that the only time you need a generator on a location is when you need a substantial amount of light.

Figure 4.2—Mounting a generator on a truck

Transformers

Some High Definition equipment runs on 100 VAC not 110 VAC, so a transformer may be required. Check the power requirements of a piece of equipment of which you are unsure. A piece of gear designed to run at 100 VAC that is plugged into a 120 VAC power source probably won't work for very long.

Inverters

With the exception of the Sony HDD–1000 VTR, virtually every piece of High Definition video equipment can be easily powered by batteries and an inverter.

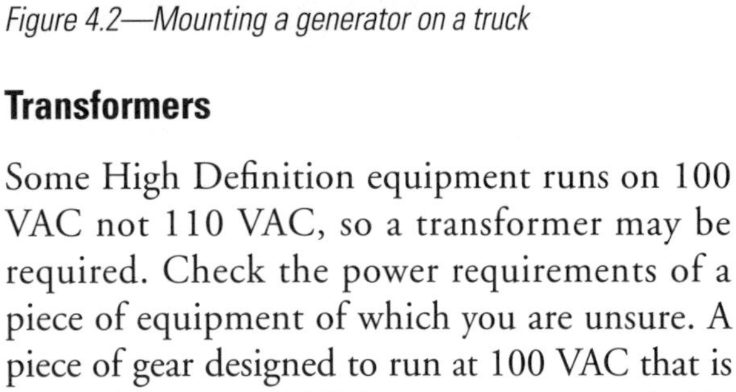

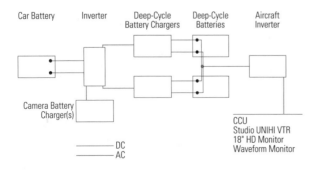

Figure 4.3—'Perpetual motion' inverter and battery schematic

Figure 4.3 is a simplified schematic for powering a system using one 12 volt and one 28 volt aircraft inverter, two deep-cycle batteries, and two deep-cycle battery chargers. The configuration illustrated is designed for use in an engineering truck, and can power almost any transportable or portable package and charge camera batteries indefinitely, as long as the vehicle's engine can be kept running.

Deep-Cycle Batteries

12 volt deep-cycle batteries, in conjunction with an inverter, can be used to power virtually any piece of equipment designed to operate on AC power. A deep-cycle battery is designed to work until the minimum operating voltage, usually 10 volts, is reached—without damaging the battery. Standard car batteries, on the other hand, are designed to deliver power only at ignition, and then to be constantly charged by the vehicle's alternator.

Figure 4.4—Batteries, chargers, and inverters

Deep-cycle batteries, often referred to as marine batteries, can be found in most auto parts stores.

Table 4.6 on page 55 shows estimated battery life for 12 volt deep-cycle batteries rated at 100 amp hours, at various current loads. The estimated life figures are not linear; higher current draws shorten battery life. Not all deep-cycle batteries are rated at 100 amp hours; higher or lower ratings will affect battery life correspondingly.

Load (amps)	Estimated life	
	12 volts	24 volts
60	~1 hour	~ 2 hours
30	> 2 hours	> 4 hours
15	> 4 hours	> 8 hours
Note: 100 amp-hour rated batteries.		

Table 4.6—Estimated deep-cycle battery life for various working loads

To calculate the power requirement for the inverter, multiply the current draw (in amps) by the AC voltage, divided by the battery voltage, and add a fudge factor to account for the inefficiencies of the inverter. For example, a piece of equipment that draws 5 amps at 120 VAC will draw about 60 amps at 12VDC.

One reason to use an aircraft-type inverter is that they are designed to operate at 28 volts. Wiring two 12 volt batteries in series halves the current draw, more than doubling battery life.

Sealed Gel-Cell Batteries

Twelve volt sealed gel-cell batteries can be used to power any piece of High Definition equipment that is designed to operate on DC power. Sealed gel-cell batteries are not only preferred over standard lead-acid batteries, they must be used any time an aircraft is involved anywhere in a shoot. Aviation regulations prohibit the transportation or shipment of lead-acid batteries on commercial and private aircraft.

Bricks and Battery Belts

Standard Anton Bauer-type bricks and battery belts can be used to power any High Definition video camera. Depending on a number of factors, including ambient temperature and which camera is being powered, they can last anywhere from 30 minutes to one hour.

BP-90 Batteries

BP-90 batteries can power the Panasonic portable UNIHI VTR and run it for perhaps 15 to 20 minutes. However they are much more suitable, with the proper adapters, to smaller pieces of equipment such as small monitors, downconverters, etc.

Cabling

High Definition video systems are six times more sensitive to timing differences than standard definition video systems are. In practical terms, this means that the total end-to-end length of all of the G, B, and R cables in a system must match to within less than *eighteen inches*, to keep pixels aligned to within 10%. (One HDTV pixel equals about thirteen feet of cable.) Otherwise pixel smearing will become visible, an effect that is cumulative.

YPbPr cabling is not quite as sensitive to timing differences as GBR cabling since Pb and Pr are each half-bandwidth signals. But, irrespective of whether you're working in GBR or YPbPr, it just makes good engineering sense to try to keep cable lengths as closely matched as possible.

Many pieces of High Definition video equipment use custom cables with custom connectors. For example, the Panasonic camera uses a custom 100 meter multicore cable between the camera and remote operations panel. Because of the small number of these cameras, finding a replacement for the cable if it goes down on location is usually impossible.

Table 4.7 compares the video input and output formats, and video and audio connectors that are used in currently available High Definition VTRs.

VTR	Video Input(s), Output(s) Connectors
Sony HDD–1000	RGB, YPbPr BNC
Sony HDV–10	RGB, YPbPr BNC
Panasonic AU–1500 (studio)	RGB, YPbPr BNC
Panasonic AU–1400 (portable)	YPbPr BNC, 26-pin VTR cable
JVC SR–W320U	YPbPr RCA

Table 4.7—VTR audio video input and output format and connectors

When the camera cable died (the blue channel developed an intermittent fault) on the first location of a four day shoot, no replacement could be found and it became necessary to try to repair the multicore cable with its custom connectors—always a chancy proposition. And as is often the case, the manuals were mainly in Japanese, and the biggest problem was to simply find the cable pin-out diagram! Once located, the problem turned out to be a failed solder joint at the connector itself (probably as a result of inadequate strain relief), which could be repaired easily, because luckily the affected wire was on the outside of the connector.

There have been reports of problems (pins being pushed in) occurring with the camera cable connectors on the multicore cables. Care should be taken to protect the connectors when not in use and when actually mating the cable. There do not seem to be these same problems with the connectors used in Sony's fiber-optic camera cable system.

The kind and quality of cabling used affects the maximum distance that multicore cables can be run. In general, 250 meters is the maximum realistic run for a copper camera cable before it becomes unwieldy to use and noise becomes an issue. Sony's fiber-optic system supports cable lengths in excess of 1000 meters. This cable is also immune to EMI and RFI problems and is very quiet, but requires additional hardware at both the camera and engineering end.

Radio Frequency Interference (RFI)

High Definition video systems, especially cameras and cables, seem to be very susceptible to RFI. REBO crews have often run into problems with RFI, especially in metropolitan locations like New York City.

While it always a good idea to check cable and system grounds, the camera and the cables themselves are acting as antennae, which can make curing RFI problems extremely difficult.

Moving the camera a few feet (if possible) or rerunning the camera cable can reduce or eliminate the problem. A case that illustrates this point dramatically occurred during a shoot where the storyboard called for a night shoot that necessitated hiring a generator and grip truck. Parking and security restrictions at the location required that the camera cable and the power cables for the lights be run parallel to each other for quite a distance and cross over each other in several spots. When the lights were turned on, there was noticeable RFI in the engineering monitor. Fixing the problem required rerunning both the camera and power cables to separate them and to keep them from crossing each other. We got lucky in this case; it's not always possible to do this.

When the source of the RFI is overhead power lines or some other emissive source (like a microwave antenna), finding a solution to the problem is not as easy. Again, moving the camera and changing the orientation of the cable can help, but not always. Replacing the multicore copper camera cables with fiber-optics can also help. Sony's fiber-optic system, which works only with their HDC–500 and HDC–300 cameras, is essentially immune to EMI and RFI problems.

Other things commonly found near a High Definition video camera that can induce EMI and RFI problems include a poorly grounded or shielded camera head that comes in contact with other metal, including a tripod, or jib arm. Sometimes the zoom cable or the camera operator can be the source of the problem.

Walkie Talkies and Intercoms

As discussed in the previous section, High Definition video cameras and cables are very susceptible to RFI and other forms of interference. One common piece of production gear that can cause problems is the walkie talkie, because many frequencies commonly used in walkie talkies seem to be right in the frequency range that High Definition camera heads and cables seem to be most sensitive to. Keying the walkie talkies can cause visible glitches in the video.

The workarounds for this are to:

1 Experiment with walkie talkie brands and channel settings to determine which, if any, cause problems, and if possible do this beforehand, not during a shoot when it can cause a real problem;

2 Use lower power walkie talkies;

3 Maintain good walkie talkie discipline and never key them during takes;

4 Use cabled intercoms; or

5 Avoid communicating on the set.

Option 1 is always the best alternative, because it is preventive in nature: addressing a potential problem before it becomes an actual problem. However, this is not always possible, especially on location with rental walkie talkies. In this case, options 2 and 3 may provide the most workable alternative solutions.

Cabled intercoms, option 4, are not always a viable alternative, especially when portability is an issue. Even on interior locations when cameras are wild, the added burden of the additional intercom cable can be a real problem.

Option 5 is *not* recommended.

Finally, while the Sony HDC–500 and HDC–300 do have voice communications (comm) built into the camera, there have been reports that they are not as good as they need to be to provide good communications.

Jib Arms, Dollies, Cranes, Motion Control Systems, and Steadicam

There are only two special considerations concerning using High Definition cameras in the above situations. The first has to do with weight, and the second has to do with monitoring.

The Sony HDC–300 is fairly big and heavy for a video camera, so it is a good idea to check with whoever is supplying the jib, dolly, crane, or motion control system to make sure that the rig can handle the camera and that there won't be excessive bouncing or torquing, especially when an arm is extended to its fullest length.

Figure 4.5—The Sony HDC–500 on a dolly

While Steadicam operators are known for their strength, the HDC–300 is really too big to be carried for extended periods of time comfortably. The HDC–500 has been used successfully on Steadicam rigs, as has the Panasonic camera.

Figure 4.6—The Panasonic AK–HC900 camera on a Steadicam

Video monitoring for the camera operator can be a problem using some of the rigs described above, specifically those that provide integral monitoring capability: there is not standard definition video output from the camera. There are three approaches to solving the problem:

1 Rig a battery-powered, portable High Definition to NTSC downconverter at the camera.

   Battery-powered, portable High Definition to NTSC downconverters are difficult to come by, and there is probably not a video output on the camera that you can use. This makes this solution a little problematic, and the addition of another battery-powered device that the camera operator needs to worry about should probably be avoided.

2 Send a downconverted signal back from the engineer.

   The High Definition video signal is sent from the camera to the engineering position, downconverted there, and sent back to the camera position via a standard video cable. This is how video monitoring is normally provided, especially for Steadicam rigs.

3 Rig a High Definition video monitor.

   When it is possible to rig a High Definition monitor at the camera position, the High Definition video signal is sent from the camera to the engineering position, split or looped through, and then sent back to the camera position.

Portable Rigging

A hand truck or other mobile device can be used for the portable configurations. In these configurations, it is possible to record while on the run, as was done in the production *Dog Day in Manhattan.*

Figure 4.7—A typical portable rig on location in Vietnam

Panasonic doesn't recommend recording in anything other than the horizontal position. Also, it is critical that the VTR be cushioned from the cart to isolate it from vibration when moving. Sorbothane foam, though expensive, is ideal for this purpose.

Figure 4.8—A helicopter rig

Special Effects Compositing (Green/Blue Screen)

High Definition video is well known for its suitability for use as a medium for special effects compositing, in part because of its ability to perform the composites in real time.

Lighting for Special Effects Shooting

The low sensitivity of the Sony HDC–100 and HDC–300 cameras made lighting the background evenly quite difficult. Not only was it more difficult to light evenly, but the extra light caused bounce and lens flare problems.

Lens flare problems surfaced in disagreements between the DP, who was metering the light on the set, and the engineer, who was looking at the scene on a waveform monitor. Using the light meter, the background might appear to be evenly lighted when the waveform monitor reported substantial variations in light levels. The differences were found to be a result of internal lens flare. In this case, what the waveform monitor reported was more important, because it represented the signal that was going to be recorded and used to generate the key signals.

With cameras of increased sensitivity, and the corresponding reduction of the light required, these internal lens flare problems have been substantially eliminated. However, the lesson remains: whenever possible, use a waveform monitor to assess the lighting's evenness when shooting green or blue screen for special effects compositing.

For more discussion on special effects compositing see *John Alonzo* beginning on page 109, *Mark Forker* beginning on page 120, and *Neil Smith* beginning on page 132; as well as *Leaves Home* beginning on page 80, *Pop Tops* beginning on page 81, *Performance Pieces* beginning on page 84, *The Pigeon Man* beginning on page 86, *Fool's Fire* beginning on page 89, and *The Astronomer's Dream* beginning on page 92.

Monitoring

Adequate monitoring equipment should be considered an absolute necessity when engineering High Definition video, except in situations where extreme portability is the primary concern and/or there are serious size and weight restrictions because of the nature of the location.

At a minimum, monitoring equipment consists of a video monitor and headphones for the audio. Where possible, a waveform monitor should also be used.

Finally, some sort of electrical/electronic monitoring device, such as a digital multimeter should also be standard equipment on a shoot. REBO engineers regularly use digital multimeters to test the remaining charge in a set of batteries and the actual voltage of an AC power supply on location.

Monitoring Video Quality

The bigger it is, the better the monitor is for assessing signal and picture quality. An 18" monitor should be considered the minimum usable monitor size for making critical judgments of image quality when shooting High Definition video. Monitors smaller than 18" simply aren't capable of displaying all of the information contained in the High Definition video signal. In fact, many engineers consider the 18" monitor too small to make critical quality judgments, preferring to use a 28" monitor. Budget and location requirements will ultimately determine whether or not using a large (18" or 28") monitor is feasible.

Figure 4.9—Typical engineering handtruck from New York: On The Edge

Unfortunately, using a large monitor is not always possible—for example, when working with a portable production package and mobility is important. In these instances, a battery-operated 9" monitor like the Ikegami HTM-1003 can be used.

While many types of noise, for example RF, simply aren't visible on small High Definition monitors unless they are exceptionally bad, small monitors nevertheless can be used to make accurate judgments concerning color, framing, and exposure. A 9" High Definition monitor was used almost exclusively during production of *New York: On The Edge*.

Whenever possible, take a waveform monitor along, and cable it in such a way as to make it possible to monitor both the output of the CCU (the input to the VTR) and the output of the VTR on both the video monitor and the waveform monitor. One way to do this is shown in Figure 4.10 .

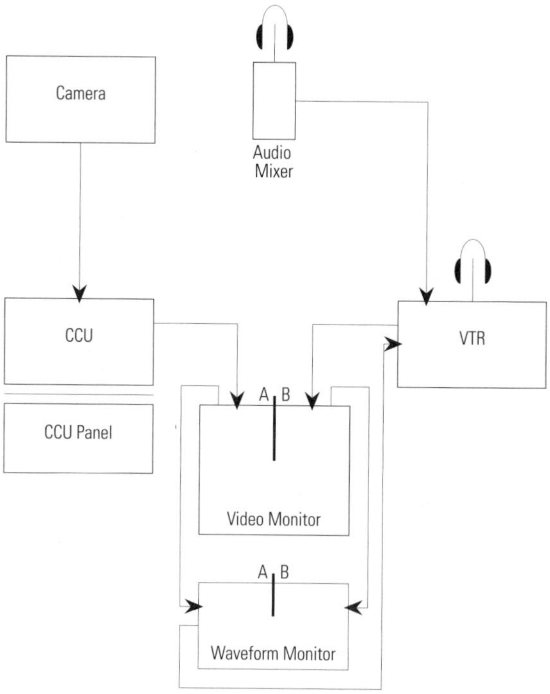

Figure 4.10—Cabling a waveform monitor into a production package

It is possible to bypass the step of monitoring the video before it goes into the VTR by sending the output of the CCU directly into the VTR and only monitoring the output of the VTR. This is risky because you're not looking at the output of the camera directly. When working this way, it is important to pay special attention to the VTR itself, especially with respect to gain settings

REBO engineers almost never go out on a location without *some* way to monitor video quality before, and as it is being shot. However, during a production there may be individual scenes that are shot without any monitoring, for example, if the camera were to be used in a tracking shot mounted to the hood of a car that was not being towed, and the engineer couldn't hide anywhere in the vehicle.

REBO engineers, however, often go out on location without a VTR that has playback capability. In almost two years of shooting with the Panasonic AU–HD1400 portable UNIHI VTR there have been only two incidences of problems with the VTR, neither of which affected the quality of the footage.

One way to resolve the playback issue is to provide the capability to check playback elsewhere. If you can afford to take the risk and the time, tapes could be sent to a studio to be checked and verified.

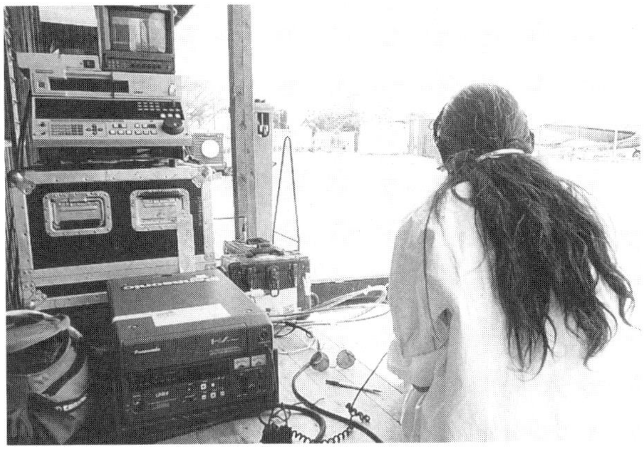

Figure 4.11—A studio UNIHI provides confidence playback on location in Kenya

Another option is to bring the necessary equipment for playback and checking on location and to set them up in a hotel room or elsewhere to provide a more timely opportunity to confirm good recordings.

A battery-powered High Definition to NTSC downconverter *can* be used to look at a picture on an NTSC monitor. This level of monitoring does virtually nothing to assure a quality recording. It is not a particularly good solution for making critical assessments of video quality. In no way is a downconverted NTSC picture sufficient for making detailed analyses of a High Definition signal/picture.

Figure 4.12—Monitoring HD video with a 4" NTSC monitor

It probably won't be possible to see RFI problems unless they are exceedingly bad. It is just enough to let you know that there is exposed and framed video getting from the camera to the VTR.

Audio and Audio Monitoring

There are no significant differences between field audio production for High Definition video and for film or standard definition video, unless the High Definition video needs to be integrated with NTSC in the course of a live production.

For more on this issue, refer to *High Definition/ Standard Definition Compatibility Issues* following.

Figure 4.13—Recording audio in the field in France

REBO productions almost always have two sets of ears monitoring audio quality during production—the audio person handling the microphone mixer, as well as the engineer. Headphones that provide good audio isolation are important for this purpose, especially when the engineer is in a high ambient noise environment.

Table 4.8 shows audio formats and input and output connectors for currently available VTRs.

VTR	# of Channels Audio Format	Video Input(s), Output(s) Connectors
Sony HDD–1000	8 PCM	Analog and digital XLR
Sony HDV–10	4 PCM	Analog XLR
Panasonic AU–1500 (studio)	4 PCM	Analog XLR
Panasonic AU–1400 (portable)	2 PCM	Analog XLR
JVC SR–W320U	Stereo Hi-Fi Monaural	Analog RCA

Table 4.8—Audio capabilities of HD VTRs

High Definition/Standard Definition Compatibility Issues

This section was originally written by Charles Pantuso, a Founding Partner and Director of Engineering, HD VISION, Inc., and was edited with his assistance for inclusion here. For additional information on many of the issues surrounding integrating High Definition video and NTSC video and audio in live, multicamera production, refer to "Woodstock '94: Live Multicamera Production Integrating High Definition Video and NTSC" beginning on page 100.

When the original 525-line black-and-white television system was modified to include compatible color information, the field rate was changed from exactly 60 fields/second (the same as the power-line frequency) to 59.94 fields/ second. This was done so that the new color subcarrier would not cause interference with the audio subcarrier, and also to a lesser extent, to mask the interference between the color subcarrier and high frequency luminance information.

As the new High Definition Television system was being developed, it seemed logical to return the vertical field rate back to its original 60 fields/second, since HDTV has no color subcarrier. This would make timecode in sync with real time and eliminate the need for drop frame timecode. There were also political reasons for returning to 60 fields/second that relate to ease of conversion to PAL, versus conversion to NTSC.

Real world integration between High Definition video and NTSC/PAL has proven that this return to 60 fields/second was a mistake. Since most programming produced for High Definition video in the near future will have as its primary market NTSC and PAL distribution, it is important to deal with these issues now, before mixed High Definition video/standard definition video production becomes more widespread. Indeed, NHK (the Japanese public broadcaster) intends to produce the 1998 Winter Olympics entirely using High Definition video cameras, and as a concession to world broadcasters and a convenience to themselves, they will operate all High Definition video equipment at 59.94. Although operating at 59.94 is a nuisance, broadcasters have a lot of experience dealing with it and can seamlessly shoot and post NTSC without any problems attributable to the vertical field rate.

The commonly used techniques for dealing with the different frame rates of NTSC (59.94 fields/second—29.97 frames per second [fps]) and SMPTE 240M High Definition video (60 fields/second—30.00 fps) are both well known and generally effective. Many productions, in Japan and in the United States, have been effectively realized in spite of this incompatibility. Most High Definition VTRs can play back at the NTSC frame rate for downconversion, and some downconverters will operate at either rate. Cameras and production switchers generally operate only at 30.00 fps.

Most current High Definition to NTSC converters perform live conversion by discarding one High Definition video field every 16.67 seconds. This causes the NTSC video to slowly drift out of sync with respect to the original audio and time code, returning to in sync about four times a minute. The actual discarding of a field causes a temporal disturbance that may or may not be objectionable, depending on picture content. The field-drop process can also create an obvious spatial resolution change if the de-interlace algorithm in the converter is not sophisticated. There are now more expensive converters that store multiple NTSC frames and only discard frames when a camera switch or static image occurs. Although this technique removes most temporal disturbances, it allows for even greater slip between the NTSC picture and original audio and time code; and if the converter is fed an isolated camera feed that never switches or stops moving, the delay between video and audio can build up to the maximum delay of the converter (as much as 30 frames) before a picture drop *must* occur due to an out-of-memory error. The converter delay will then be about one second and can stay that way indefinitely, dropping frames at the same rate as the common converters. Clearly, this approach is unacceptable, so single-frame delay converters are used almost exclusively. Even temporal interpolation converters do not resolve the lack of a one to one relationship between frames in the original material and in the converted product. This problem can make postproduction tedious.

The audio delay slip problem described above may seem trivial at first glance, but when added to the indeterminate slip of a one- or two-frame synchronizer, plus the fixed delay of one or more digital effects processors, the audio offset can be visible—and variable. Common solutions often use digital audio delays manually adjusted to compensate for the combined video delay, an approach that requires a diligent audio operator and technical director to keep track of the video path in order to maintain an acceptable lip sync error.

The solution adopted for use in *Woodstock '94* was to control the video path as much as possible and to insert a fixed audio delay close to the maximum predicted delay. This approach was chosen because audio delay is less obvious than video delay, and because automatic delay corrections can be audible in a music program. Of course, any audio delay causes slap-echo to occur between the actual live audio that is leaking into the mobile unit acoustically and the program audio monitors. This echo is also very audible to the camera people and any talent fitted with IFB earpieces.

There are other timecode and audio issues in the mixed-mode environment. Not the least of these is the inability to digitally transfer 48 kHz digital audio from High Definition digital recorders to an NTSC recorder or R-DAT recorder when the high definition recorder is playing at 59.94 fields/second. This is the preferred frame rate for nonlive conversions since no frames need be dropped. Direct digital audio transfer (without sample rate conversion) cannot take place because high definition recorders lock 48.000 kHz audio to the 60.00 fields/second vertical rate, but NTSC recorders lock 48.000 kHz audio to the 59.94 fields/second rate.

Until all High Definition video equipment can be operated at both 59.94 and 60.00, frame rate conversion will continue to be a problem when High Definition video and NTSC/PAL have to coexist during a live production.

House Standards

The following are REBO Studio's/HDLA's house standards for SMPTE 240M HDTV production.

Horizontal Blanking Interval	
Tri-level horizontal sync pulses	
Horizontal blanking width:	3.77µs ± .04µs
Vertical Blanking Interval	
Total number of lines:	45/field
Aspect Ratio	16:9
Total Scan Lines	1125
Active Scan Lines	1035
Vertical Rate	60 Hz
Horizontal Rate	33.75 kHz
Video Levels for Program Material, (analog GBR)	
Black level	0 millivolts min. (0%)
White level	700 millivolts max. (100%)
Horizontal sync tip level	±300 millivolts
Color Bar Reference Signal, (analog GBR/full bar signal)	
Black level	0 millivolts min. (0%)
White level	700 millivolts max. (100%)
Horizontal sync tip level	±300 millivolts
Time Code	SMPTE standard, NON drop frame recorded at 30 Hz vertical rate
Audio Reference Signal	1 kHz tone at –18db /+4dbm
Audio Level Headroom	18 db
Digital Audio Standard	AES/EBU format

Chapter 5

Postproduction

There are actually only three significant differences between High Definition video postproduction and standard definition video postproduction:

1 A High Definition edit is going to take longer.

The technical requirements of High Definition video are more demanding than standard definition video. Flaws that would be invisible in NTSC or PAL—even when the post is done in D1—can become glaringly visible in High Definition video. Therefore, it is necessary to be much more meticulous about quality control during all stages of the production process in High Definition video.

Another major factor to take into account is that 1" High Definition video digital VTRs are slower than their standard definition video Type-C open reel and cassette VTRs; it takes about 8 minutes to completely wind a reel of High Definition tape end to end. This is primarily because of the sheer amount of tape on a one-hour reel, more than three times what is on a one-hour 1" Type-C reel. In a machine room with a limited number of VTRs, a program with a large number of source reels, and an EDL that draws material from many reels and widely spaced timecode locations, a significant amount of time can be spent simply shuttling tape.

To a large extent, the tape shuttling problem can be solved in an interformat room where most of the source material is taken from UNIHI cassette-format VTRs, and intermediate elements and the final program is assembled on 1" digital VTRs. As long as the UNIHI cassettes are masters and not dubs, there is virtually no visible distinction between programs edited this way and programs mastered on UNIHI format and dubbed entirely to 1" digital and then edited. It is also less expensive to edit this way.

2 Most of the effects and other postprocessing equipment that is taken for granted in standard definition video postproduction either does not exist, or is very expensive—even when compared to the cost of other High Definition video production and postproduction equipment.

There are few graphics systems, few character generators, few color correctors, few digital disk storage devices, few keyers and compositing devices, and not very many digital video effects devices. Going into a state-of-the-art High Definition video online suite in 1995 has been likened to going into an NTSC online room during the early 1980s.

The fact that there are very few digital video effects devices, and even fewer edit suites that have them, means that special effects need to be very carefully designed. Unless you are planning to do your postproduction in Japan or Los Angeles, virtually all effects that required DVE-type effects will have to be done in camera or frame-by-frame using a computer graphics system.

3 It is necessary to pay attention to the time base of the various different audio and video sources.

High Definition VTRs are designed to record and play back at exactly 30 fps. When played back at this rate, digital audio is played at 48 kHz. When locked to an NTSC sync signal during the video downconversion process, the VTR cannot output digital audio at 48 kHz. Furthermore, in order for the slowed down, analog audio and timecode to remain perfectly in sync with the video, they need to be delayed by the same amount that the video downconverter causes.

The analog versus digital audio issues are not usually a problem when the audio is being used for reference only, and the audio mix is not being done in the offline, however, the delay is always an issue. Problems can arise when mixing a variety of audio sources at different sample rates and time bases. There are no insurmountable problems here, but it is important to pay attention to the various time base differences and communicate with all members of the postproduction team in order to avoid problems that will be time-consuming, and expensive, to fix.

Offline Editing

In the very early days of HDTV postproduction, all editing was done online. There was no HDTV offline system and no HDTV to NTSC downconverter that addressed the frame rate differences between HDTV and NTSC, which would make it possible to use an NTSC offline system. You can imagine how expensive and time–consuming that was.

To reduce the cost and time required for editing, REBO developed its own HDTV to NTSC downconverter (the ReScan™) that addressed the video frame rate issue (see *Downconverting High Definition Video for Offline Editing*, following). REBO then pioneered the use of digital NTSC, nonlinear offline editing for HDTV postproduction when it became one of the earliest beta test sites and one of the first purchasers of Avid's first Media Composer system.

Assuming that the frame-rate difference issue is addressed during downconversion, any computer-based, nonlinear editing system can be used.

The final result of the offline edit process is an electronic edit decision list (EDL). The EDL is transferred, usually via floppy disk or network, from the offline editing system to the edit controller in the online edit suite. If the downconversion from HDTV to NTSC was done properly, the EDL will be frame accurate. If not, the amount of work that needs to be done to fix the problem depends largely on the style the piece was edited in—especially with respect to the number of edits and the lengths of individual scenes.

Downconverting High Definition Video for Offline Editing

When downconverting video material originated in HDTV to NTSC for offline editing, it is important to take into account the slight differences in frame rate (one-tenth of one percent) between HDTV (30 fps) and NTSC (29.97 fps). This is done by feeding the High Definition VTR an NTSC-rate sync signal, effectively forcing it to play back at 29.97 fps instead of 30 fps. During the process of downconverting, the High Definition VTR is locked to NTSC sync resulting in a frame-accurate downconvert. This means that the EDL generated by the NTSC offline system will match, frame for frame, the original HDTV source material.

Analog audio is transferred, delayed by the amount caused by the downconverter.

Downconverting High Definition video to standard definition video tends to hide many kinds of imperfections, such as RFI, camera noise, soft focus, and fine detail. This is actually an advantage if the finished program is for release only in standard definition video; some imperfections simply disappear. It *can* be a big problem when the EDL generated in the offline will be used to online in High Definition for release on High Definition video or film. Because subtle imperfections might be masked, the editor might select a shot that is actually unusable. Shot selection can also be impaired because small details are not as visible in standard definition video as they are in High Definition video. This can make it more difficult to select a shot from takes that are only subtly different. (For more information, see *Transferring Film to High Definition Video* beginning on page 71.)

These potential problems provide compelling reasons for taking accurate notes during production. During takes, the engineer or an assistant can write notes, such as, 'Bad RF in shot from [timecode location] to [timecode location].' The editor can then refer to these notes during the offline.

Graphics

When REBO began HDTV production in 1986 it did not have any capability to integrate computer graphics into its production. Both Quantel and Symbolics developed, very early on, HDTV-compatible versions of their products, but these were expensive and usable only for offline graphics production. They were not designed to be integrated, unsupported, into an online production environment.

This shortcoming provided the impetus for REBO Research to develop its own graphics system, but until it was ready in 1989, titles were typeset and animated using a computer controlled animation stand.

REBO Research's ReStore™ graphics system is a dual-buffer framestore with real time digitizing, digital mixers, alpha channels, and global color correction capability. Importantly, the ReStore was designed from the beginning to be a broadcast production device, so it and its accompanying software were designed to address issues not met in most existing High Definition video edit suites.

The ReStore's host computer is a NuBus-equipped Apple Macintosh computer (680x0 or PowerPC), and it is designed to appear to the Macintosh and all software as just another monitor. In fact, when installed, it shows up in the Monitors control panel. Because of this, virtually any off-the-shelf graphics program that runs on the Macintosh can be used to create and/or manipulate images for High Definition video use.

When creating computer graphics for transfer to High Definition keep in mind that the maximum values for R, G, or B may not be 255. Some systems (the ReStore for example) set the maximum RGB value lower than 255 to allow for some headroom. This might be an issue when transferring frames created on a Silicon Graphics computer using Discreet Logic software to High Definition video via the ReStore. The artist(s) creating the graphics should be made aware of the maximum RGB value of the ReStore to avoid less than perfect results in the transfer.

Titling Using the ReStore

Adobe Illustrator and Adobe Photoshop together are an effective combination for creating titles. Illustrator is used to create object-oriented, resolution-independent EPS images that are then rasterized (converted into pixels), in Photoshop, at the correct resolution.

To create a graphic, first create a 16:9 unfilled, unstroked bounding reference rectangle in Illustrator. One that is 8" wide by 4.5" tall is convenient; each graphic fits on one 8.5" by 11" piece of paper, which can be easily printed on any PostScript printer for proofing and approval. If the finished program will also be shown in 4:3, a reference template that contains an NTSC safe title/safe action grid can easily be constructed. Illustrator is preferred over Photoshop for titling because it has extensive text handling capabilities—such as kerning—that make it possible to create professional quality titles.

Depending on the effect desired, the background rectangle in the Illustrator drawing is either filled with a color, or left transparent if it is going to be composited on top of a still picture. When titling over motion video, high-contrast titles can be created and a luminance keyer used to key the graphics over the video and add color to the text. It is also possible to construct RGBA (alpha) images in Photoshop and use the alpha channel output of the ReStore to provide the key signal to the keyer.

Once approved, the title files created in Illustrator are opened in Photoshop and rasterized at the desired resolution. Even though the image was created on a computer that uses square pixels, using a program that assumes square pixels, the rasterizing process creates an image that is the correct aspect ratio for display on the HDTV monitor, even though HDTV pixels are not square. The object-oriented Adobe Illustrator image is created in the correct aspect ratio, and the process of rasterizing the image in Photoshop creates an image that is the correct aspect ratio for the chosen display device.

A wonderful benefit of working this way is that the artwork created using this technique can be used for any 16:9 video format; HDTV, ATV, or widescreen PAL or NTSC at *any* resolution.

Macintosh/ReStore Graphics and Titling Tips

Graduated Fills

Don't use Illustrator to create graduated fills. They take forever and a week to render at High Definition video resolution. Instead, use the graduated fill capability in Photoshop. If necessary, create an image in Illustrator that contains just the object that will contain the graduated fill, and after it is placed in Photoshop, fill the floating selection as desired. As long as all multilayer elements are precisely registered within the same 16:9 bounding reference rectangle in Illustrator, they will be perfectly registered in the Photoshop composite.

Precision Alignment

For precision alignment for title dissolve sequences, the dual buffers and mixers in the ReStore come in handy. With the current title in the correct location in one buffer, load the title that follows into the other buffer. Set the mixers to 50%, and move the following title until it is registered properly.

An alternative approach that can be automated is made possible by another Macintosh program, Equilibrium Technologies' DeBabelizer. If the titles are high-cons and the background has an RGB value of 0, 0, 0, it is possible to use DeBabelizer's 'crop to color 0' function that will create a bounding rectangle exactly the size of the title. The ReStore can be set to automatically center images when they are loaded—which works only if you want your titles perfectly centered.

The dissolve can be triggered by a GPI event in the edit list.

Integrating Workstation 3D Computer Graphics Using the ReStore

High Definition video is a wonderful medium for combining computer graphics with live action. (See *Infinite Escher* beginning on page 83, *The Astronomer's Dream* beginning on page 92; and *Keith Melton* beginning on page 126.)

Once the final images have been rendered, they are transferred to the Macintosh to which the ReStore is connected. This transfer can be made by an Ethernet network connection, by disk, by DAT, or 8mm tape. The ReStore software can read images in the following formats: PICT (1- to 32-bit), interleaved 'raw' RGB, and its own proprietary high-speed format. Wavefront .rla files can also be read, but are an unsupported feature in the general release software. In addition Photoshop plug-ins are available that enable Photoshop to read and write images directly to either of the ReStore's two framebuffers.

Once the images have been transferred to the Macintosh, they are single frame edited to High Definition video tape using the ReStore software. Machine control is handled using Videomedia V–LAN controllers.

To make compositing easy, images should be rendered with an alpha (key or mask) channel. With a ReStore equipped with an alpha channel board, the output of the alpha channel can be sent to an external keyer to generate the matte and composite the image in one step. Alternatively, the entire computer graphics sequence can be recorded to tape and composited in a separate step.

It is not always necessary to transfer the images to a local Macintosh hard disk before transferring them to tape. If an Ethernet network connection can be established between the workstation and the Macintosh, the workstation disk can be mounted on the Macintosh desktop and the images loaded directly from the workstation disk across the network into the ReStore.

Online Editing

Remember the first rule of High Definition video postproduction:

> Everything takes longer.

The technical requirements of High Definition video are more stringent than standard definition video. Flaws that would be invisible in NTSC or PAL can become glaringly visible in High Definition video. Therefore, it is necessary to be more meticulous about quality control during the final edit. Among other things, you should plan to spend more time fiddling with the controls of your keyers. Images displayed on a 32" High Definition monitor do not lie. If you can see a problem in the composite, there is a problem. It may look small on a 32" monitor, but it will be very large on a 20-foot screen.

Things to Know

1 The Sony HDD–1000 1" digital VTRs are incapable of performing slow motion effects any faster than 33% of real time.

2 Without a DVE, performing strobing effects usually requires that each frame of the strobe be a separate event in the EDL. This is not difficult, but it is time consuming in the offline as well as the online.

Digital and Analog Postproduction

There are, in fact, very few all-digital commercial High Definition video edit suites in existence anywhere in the world. While an all-digital facility will deliver the highest quality finished product, the cost at present is enormous.

Experience shows that switching from analog to digital VTRs is the single most significant factor in improving image quality, even in complex multilayer compositing effects work; five or more layers can be accommodated with minimal visual signal degradation using the combination of digital VTRs/analog switcher/analog Ultimatte, even if the material is originated in analog UNIHI format. The key is to use analog VTRs only for mastering original material.

At HDLA (a joint venture between REBO Group and TVN Entertainment located in Burbank, CA), there are three Sony HDD–1000 digital VTRs. All of the rest of the postproduction gear, including one UNIHI VTR, a Sony Switcher, a Sierra keyer, an Ultimatte, and a REBO ReStore have analog video inputs and outputs. Except for some dubs and source reels, all video is stored on tape in digital format, but the video signals that enter and leave the VTR are analog, and all of the effects processing and switching is done in the analog domain.

Tape Reliability and Interchangeability

When using 1" tape stock (analog or digital) it is an absolute requirement that protection dubs be made for camera and edit masters. Even if 1" tape has not been subjected to rough handling or extremes of heat, it is very fragile. There is nothing like having the only copy of a camera master come unglued in the machine and become unusable. It only has to happen once.

Tape reliability is less of an issue with UNIHI tapes; they are generally more robust because the cassette shell reduces environmental exposure. And because of the cassette format, which makes it possible to remove cassettes from the VTR without having to rewind them, they are subject to fewer handling stresses.

However, there have been tape interchange problems between UNIHI VTRs from different manufacturers. Tapes recorded on one manufacturer's UNIHI VTR often display head switching glitches when played back on another manufacturer's UNIHI VTR. The incompatibility is usually visible as head switching glitches at the top of the frame.

This may just be due to early production problems, but it does point out the need, when mastering on a UNIHI VTR, to check to make sure that the tapes play back well on whatever UNIHI VTR the online edit facility you are using has.

Audio Postproduction

As with audio production techniques for High Definition video, audio postproduction issues, tools, and techniques for High Definition video are no different from standard definition video and film postproduction issues, tools, and techniques. The only place where extra care needs to be taken is when it is necessary to compensate for the differences between NTSC and High Definition video frame rates (see *High Definition/Standard Definition Compatibility Issues* beginning on page 62.)

The difference in program speed may have an effect on the audio portion of the program, especially if the audio program calls for extensive mixing and postprocessing. This is often the case when double-system audio is used. The issues are very well understood and are dealt with routinely when transferring audio between film and video.

In practice, there are few real problems that need to be overcome as long as records are meticulously kept and there is good and frequent communication between the video and audio postproduction people involved in the project, and they are aware of the potential problems involved.

Transferring Film to High Definition Video

This section was written with the assistance of Lou Levinson, Colorist at the MCA/MEI HD Telecine Research Center, and Barry Clark, President of Telenova. Lou has been involved in dozens of projects involving transferring film to High Definition video. Barry is the producer of dozens of natural history programs and other documentaries on film for PBS, the Discovery Channel, and other clients.

The development goal of the MCA/MEI HD Telecine Research Center is to make the processes involved in transferring film to High Definition video, NTSC, or PAL as alike as possible.

There are a lot of misconceptions when it comes to film scanning and getting film into the digital realm for manipulation. While there are many scanners that will generate files at 4K by 4K and even higher resolution, in practical terms the approximately 2K x 1K resolution of High Definition video is considered very practical when it comes to meeting the budget and deadline pressures of typical film-effects production projects. Although higher-resolution options are available, in practice they are rarely used, and even lower resolution image data can suffice in some cases.

Scanning film at 2K x 1K in real time is harder than it seems—the data stream that results is approximately 1.2 gigabits per second, and at the moment there a very few devices capable of recording that volume of data in real time. The Telecine Research Center uses a Sony HDD-1000 High Definition digital VTR. Using this

VTR makes it possible to transfer film at High Definition video resolution in real time, but the result is recorded on High Definition digital videotape. There are very few effects houses that are set up to use High Definition videotape directly, and converting the images on tape into a usable format makes the process no faster than non-real time scanning. While it is possible to use a real time film transfer device (a telecine) to transfer film to High Definition video for digital manipulation on computer workstations, they are most often used to transfer film to video for distribution, or to transfer film to video for real time manipulation using compositing tools such as the Ultimatte.

Non-real time scanning also has the advantage of being able to capture greater dynamic range than real time scanning. Real time scanning is limited to 8-bits per color, while non-real time scanners can capture 10-, 12-, and even 16-bits per color.

At present, telecines are more sensitive to correct film exposure when scanning at High Definition resolution than they are when scanning at NTSC or PAL resolution. This means that a correctly exposed negative is more important for High Definition transfers than they are for NTSC or PAL. Missing the exposure by two stops is much more of a problem in High Definition video than it is in NTSC, but as telecine technology matures over the next few years this will become less of a problem.

Jaguar: Year of the Cat, a one-hour special produced by Barry Clark of Telenova for WNET, NHK, and Canal+, was shot on Super 35 at 30 frames per second to achieve the highest quality images after the transfer to High Definition video.

The producers, aware of the importance of correct exposure, shot primarily on Eastman 5245 stock under very tightly controlled lighting conditions and exposed everything dead center. This made the film transfer very simple and accounted, in part, for the gorgeous look of the film in High Definition—and eventually in NTSC.

It's not always practical to transfer all of the footage shot for a project to High Definition video for offline editing, given the cost of High Definition tape stock. On *Jaguar* there were between twelve and thirteen hours of original material, and to save money, the producers decided to transfer only the selects to High Definition video. So, a best light transfer was made from film to NTSC with NTSC timecode, and Telenova did the offline edit in NTSC.

Because timecode in the best light transfer was not zeroed at the beginning of each telecine roll, and there was no timecode imprinted on the original negative from second system audio (because the film was recorded without sync audio), and because the producers assumed that the telecine would be equipped with a KeyCode reader, using the numbers from Telenova's EDL to transfer the film to High Definition video for the online represented quite a challenge.

One solution would be to install a KeyCode reader on the telecine, but that was not an option for this project. In the end, the numbers from the NTSC EDL were made usable—that is, the film selects could be reliably found—by forcing the film counter on the telecine to count in the timecode that would have been used to generate the NTSC EDL by using the POGLE system, which handles all the machine control for the telecine.

One nonobvious problem that crops up when transferring film that eventually will be distributed in High Definition to NTSC or PAL for offline editing is that the quality of the one light or best light transfers can affect shot selection during the offline edit. This is especially true when you use a nonlinear, digital editing system where the video will be compressed. For example, a bad transfer may cause much of the shadow detail to disappear, and this problem will be exaggerated when the footage is digitized for use on the offline system. The lack of shadow detail may mislead editors into believing that a shot is unusable, forcing them to choose a shot that may not be as appropriate.

The quality of the best light can also affect perception of the relative scale of objects in a scene. The ability of High Definition video to reproduce color and small detail better than standard definition video may cause editors to limit themselves when it is not necessary. The scale issue tends to be exaggerated further because High Definition video monitors are usually larger than standard definition monitors, and objects that would disappear on a 13" NTSC monitor could be very visible, and very effective, on a 28" or larger High Definition monitor. For this reason, it is wise to make sure that the film transfers made for the offline are of high quality. Using the highest quality digitizing setting (the one with the lowest compression ratio) will also help minimize scale and detail problems. Even so, when there are questions, an editor should refer to the best lights to help make difficult shot selection decisions.

Transferring a finished film to a High Definition video intermediary before downconverting it to standard definition D1 provides a way to create the very highest quality 4:3 aspect ratio D1 masters. It also creates a version suitable for standard definition widescreen video formats as well as High Definition.

There is a discernible difference in visual quality between a transfer made from a negative and one made from an IP (interpositive). There is more picture information in a negative than in an IP made from that negative because of fewer generations of reproduction, and because High Definition video is capable of reproducing more information than standard definition video. The additional picture information in the negative will be visible in the High Definition video transfer.

There is a tendency to perform color correction and other enhancements in D1, leaving the High Definition master untouched, instead of making corrections in the High Definition master. If the goal of the entire process is to make creating High Definition widescreen and standard definition 4:3 masters as simply as possible, then creating the highest quality High Definition transfer makes sense. In fact, it makes sense to create two High Definition masters, one framed specifically for widescreen distribution and one framed specifically for 4:3 distribution. This makes the downconversion process from High Definition video to standard definition video a pushbutton process, involving no additional color correction or repositioning.

When transferring a film shot in 1.85:1 to High Definition's 16:9 (or 1.78:1) there are very few framing problems given the similarity of the aspect ratios, even if letterboxing is not used.

When transferring from 16:9 to 4:3, the same techniques used to transfer 1.85:1 film to 4:3 for standard television can be used. Given that the entire film aperture (which is much taller than 1.78:1) is usually exposed, the *width* of the High Definition video composition can be matched and the headroom and footroom adjusted until the composition 'feels' about the same as the intended original composition. This means there may be greater headroom or footroom than in the original intended composition, but this compromise is the one that seems to work best for directors and DPs.

Repositioning may need to be done on a scene by scene basis to crop out production paraphernalia such as microphones cable taped to the floor, actors' marks, dollies, lighting equipment, crew, and shadows. This is, in fact, what happens now when transferring most 1.85:1 theatrical product to 4:3 for NTSC or PAL distribution.

While the biggest problem at the moment is how to record High Definition video in an affordable way—a Sony HDD–1000 VTR costs over $300,000 and tape stock costs over $1000/hour—the good news is that the telecine front end does not cost any more than what is currently considered state of the art in the NTSC and PAL world. The cost of transferring film to High Definition video (not including tape stock) is at the high end of NTSC/PAL telecine costs.

It is necessary, however, to trade some bells and whistles for the increased resolution demands of High Definition video. This means that there isn't a full palette of area-specific color correction capabilities in current High Definition telecines. Those functions just can't be performed in real time at such a high resolution right now. These capabilities are on their way, but they will be expensive at first. But real time grain reduction and real time dirt and scratch concealment are available today.

The answer to affordable High Definition video recording may be just around the corner. Panasonic debuted at 1995 NAB a prototype system that makes it possible to record a compressed High Definition video signal on a D5 recorder.

By the time High Definition video postproduction becomes more widespread than it is today, the tools will not be far behind what producers have come to expect and demand them to be for NTSC and PAL.

Transferring High Definition Video to Film

This section was written with the assistance of Milan Krsljanin, Manager, Sony High Definition Facility, Europe. Milan works to support the development of Digital Cinematography—interfacing program production with High Definition video technology. He is also in charge of Sony's European operation in charge of digitally recording High Definition video on 35mm film.

How the Images Are Formed

What distinguishes Sony's Electron Beam Recording (EBR) system from all other approaches used to transfer digital data to film is that the EBR system writes the image directly on the surface of the film, eliminating intermediate stages that affect colorimetry and resolution.

Because the electron beam is not visible light, color pictures cannot be produced directly. Like an X-ray, the electron beam can only form monochrome images. Therefore, each High Definition frame is recorded on black-and-white positive film as three monochrome images representing the R, G, and B components of the original image. The final result is a single strip, successively recorded separation.

The techniques used in the EBR are capable of creating extremely fine and sharp images on the fine grain black-and-white positive film that is used. Other approaches use either black-and-white CRTs with color filters, or lasers and prisms for imaging. The additional mechanical and/or optical steps in these imaging processes result in film images that are often not as sharp as those that can be created using electron beam recording.

The color negative is produced using an optical printer that exposes each monochrome RGB frame with the corresponding colored light to create a single color negative frame. One useful and often overlooked byproduct of the EBR imaging process is the creation of a single strip monochrome master, which is recognized in the film industry as the medium with the highest archival value.

The process of transferring High Definition video images to film via the EBR is fast, but it is not in real time. High Definition frames are imaged on the pin-registered EBR at a constant rate of one frame per second. Approximately 30 hours are required to image each hour of film at High Definition video resolution. While this imaging time may seem slow, it is as much as 30 times or more faster than other digital film imaging systems.

Frame Rate Conversion

An important aspect of the transfer process is frame rate conversion from the 30 fps of High Definition video to film's 24 fps. There are various techniques for performing this frame rate conversion. The crudest is simply to throw away every fifth field. However, this approach creates an artifact called judder—well known in film—in fast panning sequences.

Two different techniques involving offline digital image processing, with or without motion interpolation (creating new data from the existing image data), are available for addressing 30 to 24 frame rate conversion issues. Both approaches perform essentially the same task—adding different amounts of 'motion blur' to the picture. By changing various weighting factors, the process can be fine tuned to reduce the visibility of judder by adding variable amounts of motion blur that make transitions smoother. Which approach is used is a subjective decision; it is difficult to say that one approach is better than the other for all types of subject material.

The Creative Process

The EBR offers filmmakers a great deal of flexibility when it comes to transferring an edited High Definition video master to film. Each of the three primary colors, R, G, and B can be manipulated independently, with separate controls for balance and contrast, or gamma. This gives the producers, the director, and the DP one more step to affect and control the image that finally gets written to film.

Irrespective of the source of images—whether from a High Definition camera, High Definition telecine, or computer graphics—when you edit them together it is necessary to balance them all in order to achieve optimal image quality and the desired look. The easiest way to achieve this is to do all of the scene to scene gradings in postproduction and transfer an approved, color-corrected master.

Before transfer begins, the director, and/or DP, selects a few key scenes that are representative of the results they want to achieve, and a few tests are run, each with different color correction settings, or curves. It's not all that different from the way it's done conventionally, it's just that with the EBR there are more and finer controls. Once the film is back from the lab, an agreement is reached on which set of curves will be used for the final run. Producers value these tests because they raise the interactivity of the process while at the same time giving them more options to choose from—raising their level of confidence. It's not a question of saying this test is 'bad' and that test is 'good,' rather, 'Which test suits our requirements most closely?'

The interface to the color correction system is interactive and real time, and the changes can be seen on a High Definition video monitor as they are made. However, it is important to remember that there are some significant differences between the way film reproduces color and the way those same colors are reproduced on a High Definition video monitor. The monitor can be fairly well calibrated to show what the changes will look like when the film is processed, but it provides only a guide, not a guarantee.

In order to achieve high quality results consistently it is necessary to establish a close working relationship between the digital imaging facility and a film laboratory. It really is a question of linking two very different worlds. A film lab has one set of working standards and practices with its own language, and the electronic world has a different set of standards, practices, and terminology. In order to achieve good results, it is necessary to communicate in order to understand each others' worlds. That way, when something goes wrong, the problem can be located, or when the cinematographer has a special need everyone can work together to make that vision appear on film.

The Final Result

Many people are obsessed with the resolution issue and don't believe that High Definition video can create good looking images at 'film resolution,' which they think of as being 4000 pixels across the width of a 35mm frame (and a corresponding 3000 lines in 4:3 images). In practice, however, 35mm film is routinely scanned at resolutions of 2000 pixels horizontally, only marginally higher than High Definition's 1920 horizontal pixels, when producing film special effects in order to meet budget and schedule.

Definition, or sharpness, is only one attribute of picture quality, and it is wrong to use it as the sole criterion for performance assessment. Depth, color, contrast, dynamic range, noise, and dynamic resolution all contribute to the subjective quality of the pictures.

The EBR covers the entire range of the film latitude (density). Theoretically, the CCD in the Sony HDC–500 camera has a range of 11 stops. With the controls in the EBR, everything that can be recorded on High Definition tape can be faithfully reproduced on film.

Furthermore, the theoretical high resolution of the film negative has to be viewed in conjunction with the optical performance of the camera's lens, which can be compromised even more when filters and/or diffusers are put in front of the lens to create a desired 'look.'

The Society of Motion Picture and Television Engineers (SMPTE) published, in 1985, a paper entitled *Resolution Requirements of HDTV Based Upon the Performance of 35mm Motion-Picture Films for Theatrical Viewing*. Surprisingly (to some), the article states that even the best film projection of a print straight from the camera negative rarely exceeds a resolution of 700 TV lines.

When skeptics see the results that can be achieved at the resolution of High Definition video, they have trouble believing the quality that High Definition video offers when imaged on film via the EBR.

Chapter 6

Case Studies

High Definition video technology has developed dramatically over the past decade. From the introduction of the earliest production equipment in 1986 until now, the field has seen a quite rapid evolution in production tools, aided in no small part by advances in production tools for standard definition video.

The development of High Definition video equipment can be divided into eras. The equipment available during each of these eras played a definining role in determining the type of productions that could be accomplished, and each era ushered in a unique set of challenges, trade-offs, and opportunities.

The Analog Era

The early years of HDTV production were marked by the exclusive availability of analog production equipment: the Sony HDC–100 Saticon tube camera and the HDV–1000 analog VTR. All of the available postproduction equipment was also analog. Everything worked in the 5:3 aspect ratio that was the original HDTV image format.

REBO productions during those years include: music videos for Cameo, John Lennon, Herb Alpert, and Nona Hendryx with Zbigniew Rybczinski; commercials for Sony, Reebok, and Kentucky Fried Chicken; the shorts *Infinite Escher* and *Performance Pieces;* the animated short, *Televolution;* and the feature film, *White Hot.*

During this time, REBO Research debuted its ReStore™, a Macintosh-based dual-store graphics device. Using standard Macintosh graphics software, ColorStudio, Photoshop, Illustrator, and others, artists could now attempt the creation and editing of sophisticated graphics. Until the ReStore came along, titles on all REBO productions were produced the old-fashioned way: typeset and shot with a camera on an animation stand.

The Hybrid Era

The first third of the Hybrid Era of HDTV production was marked by: a change in image aspect ratio from 5:3 to 16:9; the introduction of a new camera, the Sony HDC–300 Saticon tube camera; and the introduction of a digital VTR, the Sony HDD–1000. No digital postproduction equipment became available.

The middle third of the Hybrid Era of HDTV production was marked by: the introduction of a CCD-based camera, the Sony HDC–500; an analog cassette tape format, UNIHI, and studio-sized decks for production and postproduction; and the introduction of early prototype digital video effects devices and switchers for postproduction.

The final third of the Hybrid Era of HDTV production (the period we are in now) has been marked by the introduction of portable production equipment, notably the Panasonic AK–HC900 camera and AU–HD1400 UNIHI VTR.

REBO productions during the Hybrid Era include: *The Pigeon Man; The Astronomer's Dream; Rabbit Ears; Clearwater: Celebrating the Hudson River; Copper Canyon; Dog Day in Manhattan; New York: On The Edge; Passage to Vietnam;* training classes for the Taiwan Broadcasting Development fund; and more than 50 others.

The Modern Era

This is the era we are just entering. The next few years will see the introduction of High Definition video production equipment that will combine, for the first time, the imaging capabilities and widescreen aspect of High Definition video with the portability and access to production and postproduction tools that are taken for granted in standard definition video and film production.

The Analog Era

Zbig's Visions

Some of the first projects produced by REBO were music videos for Cameo, John Lennon's *Imagine*, Herb Alpert, and Nona Hendryx, directed by Zbigniew Rybczinsky. For a description of the projects, see page 7.

White Hot

White Hot (directed by Robby Benson; Neil Smith, DP) was the first feature-length film shot on HDTV in the US, and only the second feature length film project in the world.

Making a feature film is a major undertaking, especially when you take into account the fact that production began only six months after first receiving the equipment, the project is joined during the tail end of preproduction, and there are only eight days until principal photography is supposed to begin.

White Hot was shot using the Sony HDC–100 camera, and recorded and edited on analog VTRs. The 100 pushed Saticon tube technology to its limits and was plagued with all of the problems that tube cameras are faced with and worse, including comet tailing, ghost images, low contrast, low sensitivity, and registration drift.

The low sensitivity of the 100—it was rated at 64 ASA—meant high lighting requirements. Needing that many footcandles added quite a bit of time and instruments to each lighting setup, which, in a low-budget film, is something that can't really be easily afforded.

Because the iris was nearly always wide open, depth of field became a problem. The eyepiece of the 100 made things even more difficult; it was never sharp, and focusing was very difficult. In the end, it was easier to have the engineer check focus, which slowed things down further.

The screenplay called for a hood-mounted tracking shot. Unfortunately, there was no way to simply mount a self-contained camera rig on the hood of the car, as would have been done in a 35mm film shoot. Instead, the car was towed around Manhattan by the equipment truck, which was equipped with a generator, and the camera was rigged on the car with a cable flying between the camera and the equipment truck.

Comment from DP Neil Smith

> "Was it worthwhile? We made a lot of mistakes, and we learned a tremendous amount. My only regret is that we didn't go right in and immediately do another feature. We'd made all the mistakes, and we should have capitalized on what we learned. We could have brought High Definition video production techniques and advantages to the feature film world much sooner."

Leaves Home

Leaves Home (directed by Cosimo; Neil Smith, DP), was a :30 national commercial for Sony's then-new video Walkman. The commercial opens on a wide shot of a businessman leaving for work. When he jumps into his friend's car, he looks back to see his entire house lifted off its foundation by a giant construction crane—emphasizing the portability of Sony's new product.

Figure 6.1—Still from Leaves Home

High Definition video mattework was the simplest method for solving this problem. Only two layers would be necessary: the background exterior, and a miniature house.

The miniature house would logically be the second, or top layer. This required the car entering the shot on the background element, to be below the area to be occupied by the miniature. Otherwise, it would slide under the house destroying the illusion.

The camera lens height was the same as the top of the foundation wall and 95 feet from the back of the prop stairs. The frame size was set by keying into the live camera a still scale picture of a model house from a REBO Research ReStore. The crane that was supposed to be lifting the house was just in frame on camera right, with the boom almost straight up.

The background layer was shot as the man walked down the path to the car. An air compressor blew a cloud of fullers earth upwards behind the foundation, and the crane dropped a wide dispersal of garbage from above the top frame line.

The miniature house was built to the scale of one inch to one foot. It was to lift off its foundation wall just below the clapboard siding. In the studio, the model house was placed on a miniature foundation wall of blue painted wood attached to a blue card contoured to scale, matching the gradient of the exterior background plate. Ten feet behind the table was a blue wall. All the blue was lit identically. A 10K fresnel matched the sun direction of the background plate, and bounce light from a six by six silk took care of the ambient fill.

As the miniature's scale was one inch to one foot, the camera was placed so that the focal point in the lens was 95 inches from the front door, and exactly the height of the top of the blue foundation block. Power to the interior house lights ran through the model crane hook attached to the handle on the roof. We rolled tape, the house was lifted, the gaffer made the interior lights flicker and go out.

In postproduction, the background plate with the man on the path was keyed into the blue of the miniature house. Again, the gradient made it possible to have the man below the miniature and not be covered by it. As he approached the car, the house lifted behind him, and a wipe followed the rising house making the falling garbage seem to drop from the bottom of the house.

Production was completed in three days. The ability to actually see the composite image on the HD monitor as it was being made, right on the set, took a lot of the pressure off everyone.

Pop Tops

Pop Tops (Jean-Paul Goude, director; HD consultant, Neil Smith) was a :30 commercial for Reebok. The storyboard include a number of complex live-action composites, and the agency was interested in seeing if High Definition video could help them produce the commercial more cost effectively. At the time, there was quite a bit of interest in the agency community in using High Definition for high-end commercial production, but with the introduction of D1 and real time component digital video effects devices, much of the work went that way.

Figure 6.2—The Pop Tops *set and exterior composite*

As with many other productions, the client decided to consider using High Definition only after preproduction was well under way. For *Pop Tops*, many creative decisions, especially with respect to mechanical effects design, had already been made from a film shot-for-NTSC perspective, which meant that some effects did not take full advantage of what High Definition video offers.

The basic effect was to create a shoe store that could be drenched. Using a real shoe store would be prohibitively expensive, so a set was built on a bluescreen studio. Large storefront windows actually contained glass to provide a more realistic effect.

During shooting on the interior set, meticulous notes were kept for every shot regarding lens to subject distances, boom height, focal length, boom changes, and dolly movements. Also noted were all set dimensions and prop locations.

From all of the footage shot in the studio, the director selected the takes that would be used in the edit. These shots were dubbed onto a select reel that was taken on location for the second part of the shoot.

Location scouting identified a piece of pavement large enough to chalk out a 'virtual' shoe store. The camera was then placed in this space using the notes taken from the studio, and all of the foreground shots to be composited over the 'real' shoe store were shot, using the select reel to check to make sure that all of the elements worked, including camera moves, right there on location.

In one part of the commercial, pedestrians outside the store appear to lean in and look at what is going on when the sprinklers in the store go off. A chalk line was drawn on the pavement and the talent could toe the line and lean over it, providing a strong illusion that they were actually looking into the store. Helping complete the illusion was the fact that High Definition video was able to read the subtlety of the glass that was originally recorded in the windows in the set and was preserved through the compositing process. This could not have been done in NTSC.

Figure 6.3—HD compositing realistically merges the exterior with the Pop Tops *set*

One of the mechanical effects was to have smoke coming out from one of the actor's ears. It turned out to be an expensive rig, which of course had to be invisible. During the shoot, the effect fizzled, and an impromptu replacement had to be created on the spot. The replacement was a cardboard box with a bellows attached and a smoke cookie inside. Because it was important not to lose a generation, the effect had to be performed live and composited on the set in real time. Because there was no longer a mechanical rig that could be triggered remotely, someone had to perform the effect live by pumping the bellows precisely on cue.

Figure 6.4—The final smoke effect in Pop Tops

Infinite Escher

Infinite Escher (directed by John Sanborn and Mary Perillo; Neil Smith, DP; CG house, Post Perfect) was among the first ever integrations of 3D computer animation with live action High Definition video. *Infinite Escher* is the story of a young boy (played by Sean Ono Lennon) who convincingly appears to interact within the artworks of Dutch artist M.C. Escher.

*Figure 6.5—*Infinite Escher *convincingly mixes live action and CG*

Flight

For this scene in the video it was necessary to shift Sean from a standing position to a flying position through moving computer generated backgrounds of complicated Escher architecture. At the time of shooting, only wireframe versions of the 3D environments were available.

Sean lay face down on a blue pedestal built with rounded corners and molded against the studio floor. In front of Sean was a forty foot wide blue wall, sixteen feet high with a sweep that carried the blue under the pedestal. The entire blue was soft lit from above with sky pans filling in the top of the wall.

Because Sean was stationary, the camera had to perform all the motions required to simulate a convincing flight. A Panavision Panatate was modified to mount a Sony HDC–100 camera. With this device mounted on a fluid head we could pan, tilt, and fully rotate the camera about the axis of the lens.

The Panatate set up was then mounted on a crane. The shot began with the camera rotated 90 degrees, shooting down and from one side of Sean. Sean's performance, coupled with the framing, gave the impression that he stood firmly on the ground, nonchalantly looking up at the strange world around him.

As Sean raised his arms, the camera and grip department rushed through a well-choreographed set of maneuvers, simultaneously dollying back, booming up, panning, tilting, and rotating the camera to give the effect of a convincing take-off and flight that matched perfectly to the wireframe that was running as a composite shot on the director's monitor. This shot, as with most on the production, was recorded as a blue element that became part of a computer generated environment, assembled from as many as eleven layers.

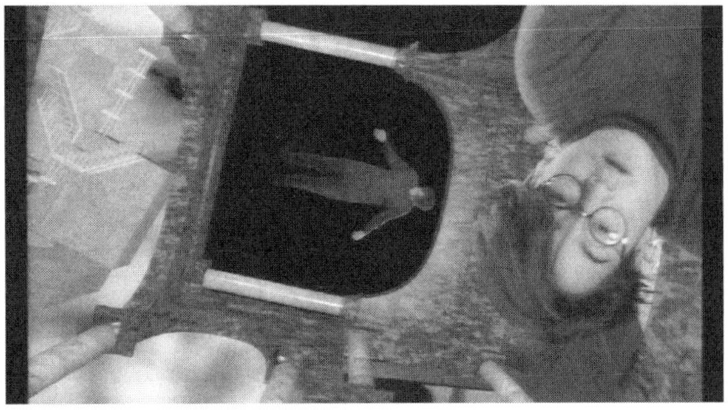

Figure 6.6—Still from the Flight segment of Infinte Escher

Hands

For this scene it was necessary to create a shot similar to that of Escher's pencil sketch of two hands drawing each other, from the boy's point of view of his drawing table.

A Sony HDC–100 camera was locked off from almost overhead. It was essential that it did not move in any way. The prop department prepared a piece of drawing paper with shirt sleeves and arms (no hands) drawn only to the wrist. This was fixed to the top of the table with double-sided tape. The table was weighted with sandbags.

Sean placed his right arm over the arm drawn at the top of the paper. His wrist was made to align as close as possible to the pencil drawn wrist (on the top of the page). We rolled the tape, and he pretended to draw the lower shirt sleeve.

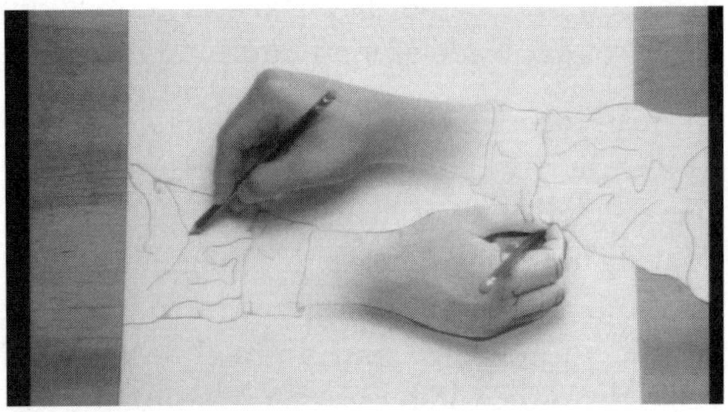

Figure 6.7—Still from the Hands segment of Infinite Escher

Sean's right hand and wrist were then treated with white makeup and black eyebrow pencil to resemble a three-dimensional drawing. He placed himself on the other side of the table and aligned his arm to the bottom drawing in the same way as he had done at the top. We rolled tape, and he again pretended to draw the other sleeve.

In postproduction, a high contrast black-and-white matte was created on the REBO ReStore graphic system. This high con divided the white left side of the screen from the black right side with an "S" shaped, soft edged line that would run above the wrist joints of both hands.

The high con was used as a wipe to softly join the left half (right-sided hand drawing left sleeve) of one shot to the right half (left-sided hand drawing right sleeve) of the other, giving the effect we required of live hands growing out of pencil drawn arms.

The result was a totally convincing illusion that has a great deal of production value, yet was very simple to execute. To execute the same effect in film, the hold-out matte would had to have been drawn on cels, shot on an animation stand, and then used in an optical printer.

Comment from online editor Mark Forker

"I wanted to put shadows on everything because the computer graphics that were rendered for the piece looked very computer graphicy. For example, nothing cast shadows. There are actually still one or two shots in the finished piece that have shadows where I was moving wipes across the screen by hand, but the fact is, it was going to take too much time to add that necessary extra bit of detail to add more realism. We realized that without hold-out mattes and some sort of digital video effects device (which didn't exist at the time) the shadows were going to be impossible. If there is a 'fault' with *Infinite Escher,* it's that the computer graphics look cool but the sophistication in terms of the integration with the live action isn't high enough to really pull it off."

Performance Pieces

The ten-minute short, *Performance Pieces* (directed by Tom Abrams; Neil Smith, DP), is the story of an outrageous performance artist (played by F. Murray Abraham) who takes Vincent Van Gogh's act of slicing off his ear a few steps further. The viewer quite convincingly sees the artist's disembodied head narrating the film from one gallery while his other body parts are seen performing on their own in famous museums around the world.

Figure 6.8—Unveiling the artist in Performance Pieces

The effect around which the whole premise of *Performance Pieces* revolved was simple—placing the live, truncated head of F. Murray Abraham on a pedestal in an art museum.

Figure 6.9—One of the artist's performance pieces

The first task was to shoot the background, including the pedestal, upon which the head was to appear. The frame sizes and focus were determined through the use of a fake head that was removed for the shot. The lens height was adjusted in each shot so that the top of the pedestal would be just out of frame, and the plane of the top would be seen only as a perfectly horizontal straight line. Notes were taken for every shot with regard to camera and lighting, focal length, distance, foot candle readings, etc.

After the backgrounds were completed, work in the studio began. Mr. Abraham sat in a chair in front of an evenly lit blue wall. He wore a tight fitting wooden collar that would appear to be the marble base for the talking sculpture. The collar was bolted to a wooden frame so that it would not move.

The camera specifications and Mr. Abraham's lighting were matched to the notes from the background location. The lens height was set to see the base of the collar as a straight, horizontal line at exactly the same placement in the screen as the top of the pedestal in the background plate.

A foreground "garbage matte," which was simply a blue card, was placed in front of Mr. Abraham's torso, one straight edge lined up with the bottom of the wooden collar. This was lit evenly so as to match the wall. Fine adjustments were made to lighting and camera while viewing live composite shots of both background and foreground elements. When the director, DP, and engineer were satisfied that they married perfectly, the finished matte shots were recorded.

Performance Pieces contains several flashback sequences. These were shot on 16mm film and processed to make them look old. The film was projected onto a sheet and rephotographed using a Sony HDC–300 camera.

Figure 6.10—A shot on film flashback in Performance Pieces

Production on the entire piece, with numerous composite shots, was completed in three days.

Performance Pieces was transferred to 35mm film and won first place at the Cannes International Film Festival in 1989 in the Narrative Short Film category.

Comment from director Tom Abrams

> "The beauty of working in this medium is that the director, the actors, and the crew could see a theoretical concept come together as it was being made. We knew we had the effect as we were recording it. It is a great psychological boost to be able to create effects at the same time you are shooting principal photography."

Televolution

Televolution (directed by Malcom McNeill) was a self-promotional piece consisting of two short animated bumpers showing the evolution of mankind from single-cell amoebas to widescreen-TV watching teenagers, and then devolving back to a single-celled life form.

Figure 6.11—The evolution of Televolution

Production on *Televolution* was done using traditional cel animation techniques with a simple twist: bluescreen was used as the background plate to make it possible to combine the drawn cels with stock effects footage, such as video snow, using an Ultimatte.

Figure 6.12—Upconverted NTSC video snow composited into Televolution

Cels were captured using a Sony HDC–100 camera, digitized into a REBO ReStore, and edited "on twos" onto a Sony HDV–1000 analog VTR.

The Early Hybrid Era

The Pigeon Man

This case study is excerpted from *Bird Brains*, a behind-the-scenes video produced by REBO about the production of *The Pigeon Man*. Participating in the discussion are executive producer Barry Rebo, writer and director Malcolm McNeill, and editor Mark Forker.

Barry Rebo

> "*Pigeon Man* was an existing script that Malcolm McNeill showed to me that he was interested in producing. We tried to find a way to produce the piece as a commission for a corporation, and we were fortunate to have NEC take the project on."

Malcolm McNeill

> "The basic idea of *Pigeon Man* is that there are millions of pigeons in New York City—but no one I know has ever seen a baby one. To me, the question, 'Why are there no baby pigeons?' is as absurd as why there are no baby televisions or baby buses. I decided that there must be some middle-aged couple living on the Upper West Side that repairs and maintains all the pigeons, in New York City, which are battery operated.
>
> "When we started working with the (real) pigeons outdoors we discovered a few things about pigeons that really surprised us. For instance, there's a whole army of elderly people that get up very early every morning with bags of food and go out and feed the pigeons. I guess it's why you not only never see a baby pigeon, you never see a thin one. Anyway, if you don't get your equipment up and running early enough, by eleven o'clock they're full up for the day, they're up in the trees, and there's no way you're going to get them down on the ground. We got lucky in Union Square when a young guy showed up with a whistle and said that he could get the

pigeons to go wherever we wanted them to. He started blowing his whistle, and sure enough, all the birds took off. It turned out that the whistle was the sound of a buzzard or a hawk or some other predator, and he was actually terrifying the pigeons. They were too scared to land anywhere. But we did get some good pictures of them flying all over the park.

Figure 6.13—Working with pigeons in the studio

"Shooting the pigeons on bluescreen was pretty straightforward. Pigeons are very smooth. They don't have hair problems or anything like that to deal with. They're pretty docile, and you can do just about anything you want with them. We shot them on the ground to insert over ground shots, and we shot them on branches to keep the illusion of being in the trees. All of the [pigeon] 'portrait' shots were done in the studio. Pigeons actually get tired very quickly, surprisingly enough, and so there were times when they just sat on the branch, and we got some good close-ups, and when we wanted them to move, we just shook the branch. And since they're four feet in the air with no wings, they get nervous very quickly because they don't really want to fall off the branch.

"But they're easy to work with; they're not really all that bright, and they don't really ask for much. But, we had to spend a lot of time cleaning the studio up afterwards.

"The shooting schedule was very tight and very specific. The three days that we shot outside we were able to get the shots we needed, but it did rain on two of the days. The skies on the last day were perfectly, evenly blue, almost Ultimatte blue, and we were able to key them out and replace them with different skies (with clouds in them) which helped give the piece a more consistent look."

Mark Forker

"High Definition video was ideal for this program because of the amount of bluescreen work involved. The storyboard called for a lot of compositing that would have to look completely transparent. We needed to put pigeons into environments realistically. They couldn't look cut out—that wasn't stylistically what we wanted.

Figure 6.14—Pigeons composited into an exterior shot

"The dream sequence was created by selecting a number of backgrounds to composite various shots of pigeons over. Some of the backgrounds were sky, which we changed the colors of by using various combinations of patching out individual RGB channels and using the color correction capability of the ReStore to change RGB levels and contrast very precisely. Maps were used for some backgrounds, and these were captured by placing a camera on an animation stand. We took the pigeons that were shot over bluescreen in the studio as well as the pigeons from location and composited them against these various backgrounds

"The 'chow-chow-chow' sequence was where the pigeons were seen going forward-reverse, forward-reverse. This was done in the traditional manner of editing two frames forward, three frames back, because the High Definition VTRs do not run backwards the way some tape machines can."

Malcolm

"At one point, the Pigeon Man sees his pigeons on a High Definition monitor in his home. The monitor in the set didn't work, so we couldn't simply rephotograph some edited footage. We needed to find a way to create the effect in post without having all of the elements we needed during the shoot."

Mark

"For a number of reasons, the High Definition TV was not shot from the reverse angle, or from what would be the Pigeon Man's point of view. The next studio shoot day the High Defintion monitor was shot in the required angle against bluescreen. Then we had to create the environment that it would exist in—and the background plate was also not shot.

Figure 6.15—Composing the Pigeon Man's view

"We used the REBO ReStore to do this. The ReStore uses off-the-shelf Macintosh software to do any number of PaintBox-style manipulation of frames. We digitized various portions of the existing environment, the wall, floors, curtains, and an artist created the necessary backgrounds plates cut-and-paste style.

Figure 6.16—Using Macintosh software to create a matte

"In order to show the beginning portion of the show in the monitor for the Pigeon Man to watch, the beginning of the show needed to be edited first. Once completed, the beginning of the show was played back in a monitor that was angled at exactly the right position, and the beginning of the sequence was rephotographed. Using a matte created in the ReStore, the background created by the artist was composited with the rephotographed video to complete the effect."

Barry

"*Pigeon Man* is a great example of a cost-effective way to produce special effects. What you see in *Pigeon Man* is a host of NEC products set out in an amusing way that shows the high quality in the execution, as well as the design of the project, and that would reflect well on NEC products."

Malcolm

"One of the unusual things about *Pigeon Man* was that NEC allowed us to produce eight minutes of video where there's not one real product shot. Everything is just integrated into the live action, and, in fact, if you didn't know it was NEC and that NEC was advertising their products, you wouldn't even think about it."

Barry

"*Pigeon Man* was conceived as a High Definition project. In fact, I think when Malcolm designed it he knew that this was another example of how you could stress the unique capabilities of High Definition video. One of the things we realized after producing *Pigeon Man* was that we had picked a project that showed the natural application of High Definiton video in service to a story.

"If you look at the special effects in *Pigeon Man*, they work not only because they're intelligent and well designed, they don't linger on the screen. There are enough of them there to trick your imagnation, but unlike earlier High Definition effects work you don't dwell on them. If you dwell on any special effect eventually you see where the magic and the strings are."

Malcolm

"The effects in *Pigeon Man* are there there to help the story. It isn't a story made up in order to show off a lot of effects, which is why the effects—when they were there—really worked. It's because they were simple, they weren't there just for the sake of it. A lot of people have seen some of the composites and not realized that the pigeons weren't actually in the scene at the time."

Fool's Fire

Fool's Fire (written, directed, and produced by Julie Taymor), an adaptation of the Edgar Allen Poe short story, *Hop Frog*, was a coproduction for the series *American Playhouse*. Although Ms. Taymor is quite well known for her work in the theater, *Fool's Fire* was her first film project.

The original intent was to shoot entirely in High Definition video, but during budgeting it became apparent that it would not be possible to realize the director's vision for the production dollars available. For this reason, it was decided to shoot all of the principal photography in 35mm film, much of the effects photography in High Definition video, and use High Definition video postproduction techniques to perform all of the complex compositing the story required.

Figure 6.17—Hop Frog and the puppet king

One of the chief creative challenges of the project was to take people with a lot of experience in a lot of different media—model makers, puppeteers, the theater, filmmakers, and High Definition video effects designers, engineers, DPs, and camera operators—and make everything look cohesive.

One of the chief technical problems the production faced was the integration of the many 35mm film elements for the special effects sequences with the High Definition video and trying to make it look seamless.

The decision was made to shoot on Eastman 5296 negative stock, which is rated at 500 ASA. Using such a fast stock made film lighting requirements minimal, making production faster and less expensive. The High Definition video camera used was the Sony HDC–300, which is rated at about 64 ASA, several stops slower than the film stock. The Sony HDD–1000 1" digital VTR was the record deck.

During postproduction, blue screen elements that were shot on film were transferred to High Definition video and composited with one or more bluescreen elements originated in High Definition video using an Ultimatte. Very few problems arose with compositing the film and High Definition bluescreen elements, but film grain did prove to be more of a problem than anticipated.

Figure 6.18—Compositing multiple film elements

For stylistic reasons, the film was shot quite dark, which meant that there were a lot of dark areas with deep shadows. When compositing, matching the High Definition video-originated material was the cause of much concern. In the end, however, there was no need to add film grain to the High Definition elements because composited elements went through so many stages that everything took on a homogenized look. After a few cycles, there was enough grain in the High Definition video-originated elements to make them match the film-orignated elements quite well.

Another unanticipated problem was fire. The production included a lot of fire, and the director wanted the flames to be orange. In order to do that, it was necessary to light things very hot, about 1200 footcandles, otherwise the flames would go white.

Figure 6.19—One of the fire shots in Fool's Fire

One of the more difficult special effects scenes was a sequence where the main character, Hop Frog, needed to appear to jump out of a window in this castle, tumble, and then disappear into another window. The director didn't want it to look photorealistic; if it could have been realistic it would have been a lot easier. A stylistic approach to the tumbling was needed. In the end the effect had a kind of stutter or step freeze look to it. This is a case where better previsualization and some testing would have helped. The elements were shot as if the effect would be realistic. With better previsualization, and knowing that a stylized effect was wanted, the effects designer, effects editor, and director would have been able to shoot the required elements in a fashion that would have helped achieve the desired effect more transparently and make it more believable.

Figure 6.20—Hop Frog's tumble, part 1

As it was, Neil Smith, the High Definition effects designer, who was also the second unit director, and effects editor Mark Forker talked off and on for weeks discussing how to shoot the scene. On location, Neil called Mark to say that the way they decided to shoot it wouldn't work. On the phone, in under an hour, they came up with a new approach.

Figure 6.21—Hop Frog's tumble, part 2

Even if there was a digital video effects device to help exaggerate the tumble in post, it might not have worked, because the lighting has to appear to be correct throughout Hop Frog's leap, and there are subtle perspective changes that happen when a camera is stationary and something moves through its field of view. Those are things that can't be easily faked using digital video effects.

In the end, Hop Frog's leap and tumble effect was done by rotoscoping the sequence using Photoshop on stills captured using the REBO ReStore. Hop Frog was cut out, repositioned, and resized as needed, but the lighting and perspective subtleties that would have contributed to the realism of the effect were not included because they could not have been done cost-effectively.

Rabbit Ears

Rabbit Ears (produced and directed by Craig Rogers; edited by Mark and Susan Forker; Mark Forker, Susan Forker, and Anna Pivarnik, motion control) is a series of 30-minute animated productions produced for Rabbit Ears Productions. Each program consisted of original illustrations for well known and not so well known childrens' stories edited together with original music and celebrity voiceover narrative.

The primary creative challenge was to take the illustrations and to bring them to life without making them look like television or conventional cel animation. The goal was to preserve what the illustrator did; not to try to overmanipulate the images or overuse optical or digital video effects. The desired end result was to make sure that a viewer would be able to "get" the story just by looking at the illustrations, without any sound. This could not be done with MTV-style music video editing, where the pictures are used to support the songs. With these productions, the audio was to support the pictures, which needed to stand on their own.

The chief creative and technical challenges on the project were to accommodate widely varying image formats and to produce a product that would work well in both 16:9 and 4:3.

Some of the illustrations were quite small and some were very large. While illustrators usually worked in roughly the same scale for an entire story, sometimes it was necessary to integrate illustrations of wildly different scales in the same story. To accomplish this feat, the production upgraded the existing capabilities of REBO's Motion Products International animation stand significantly. During this upgrade, the weight and size of the High Definition video camera needed to be taken into account, as the arm supporting the camera was extended significantly to accommodate the very large drawings used in some episodes.

Many of the productions required complex multilayering, so one more addition to the kit of tools designed specifically for the production was a light box measuring 3 by 6 feet. By placing this light box on the animation stand with the artwork on top of it, it was possible to create traveling matte elements with very large pieces of art.

Rabbit Ears' programs are viewed all over the world. Coproduction support provided the additional dollars need to produce the series in High Definition video, but conversion of the programs into standard definition video for worldwide distribution was always a part of the producer's and director's thinking.

Craig Rogers, the director on the project, also dealt with all of the artists involved, and directed them to draw the illustrations and construct their scenes in a way that would be effective in both 16:9 and 4:3. None of the really important action or focus existed on the edges of the 16:9 screen, necessitating some compromises that, fortunately, did not detract from the impact of the imagery in High Definition. Occasionally, a move would be programmed that would travel the art from one side of the 16:9 screen to the other. The center area of the art was all that could be seen in 4:3, and while the edges of the art were being used, nothing important happened on the edges only.

To aid in making directing decisions in 16:9 and 4:3, live HDTV to NTSC downconversion and the placement of a 4:3 monitor immediately above the 16:9 monitor made it possible for the director and motion control programmer to have a simultaneous view of what a move would look like in both aspect ratios. Every move could be rehearsed and the motion parameters changed until the director was satisfied with the way the move looked in both 16:9 and 4:3. Using two monitors was more effective than simply masking an expensive 16:9 monitor or drawing the edges of the 4:3 frame with grease pencil.

Many production and postproduction steps were merged during production. The director and motion control program (who was also the editor) would literally be shooting with access to the edit room, compositing in real time with the camera as a source, creating elements and their mattes, and rehearsing everything to make sure it worked. Production usually did not occur in a linear fashion according to the storyline. Instead, the difficult scenes were often worked on with the facility of a switcher or other tools in the edit room.

The justification for working this way was simple, although, perhaps counterintuitive: in the end it would cost less. Producing each program conventionally was budgeted at one week to shoot all of the individual elements and two weeks to edit the finished piece. By spending some time during production doing post work, it was possible to accomplish more than half of the post effects during the two week shoot schedule. At the end, all that was left was the simple editing of completed elements together, a task needing only a day or so to complete.

The Middle Hybrid Era

The Astronomer's Dream

The Astronomer's Dream (written and directed by Carl Colby; Neil Smith, DP; special effects supervisor, Abby Levine), is a short film for Sony Corporation's High Definition Video Software Center that dramatizes Johannes Kepler's discovery of the laws of planetary motion.

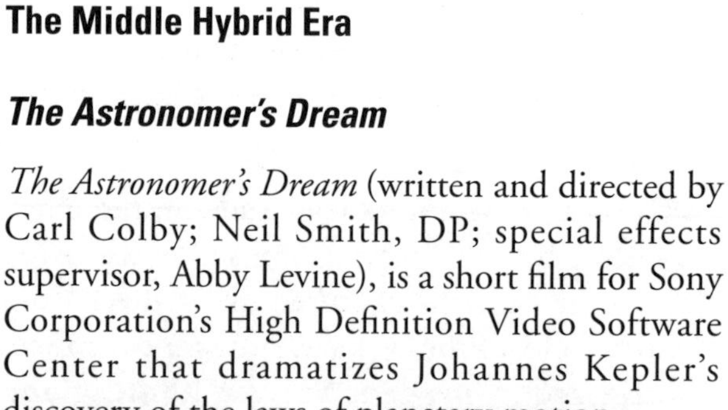

Figure 6.22—The astronomer's dream

Creating the Heavens

All of the stars were taken from text listings in the Bright Star Catalog. The Bright Star Catalog is a database that describes stars in terms of galactic latitude, longitude, and brightness. With the use of custom Macintosh software, approximately 9500 stars were extracted from this database. Then, 3D objects were created for them, and these objects were transferred to a Silicon Graphics (SGI) workstation for rendering, using Wavefront software. Each star's brightness was adjusted for best appearance on a High Definition monitor. The atmospheric twinkling was added in postproduction by looping a sequence of five frames rendered on the SGI workstation.

Creating the Solar System

Planetary Arts and Sciences (PAS) has derived full planetary surface maps from a variety of missions and data sets from NASA and JPL. They have done much of the work of eliminating the seams, distortions, and color and brightness variations found in the original data. Data from PAS was used to create the surface maps for Saturn, Neptune, Jupiter, Uranus, as well as for Saturn's rings and the clouds of Venus.

The digital data from PAS, in the form of black-and-white "raw" files of various resolutions and filtration, was supplied to REBO on 8mm Exabyte data tapes in UNIX `tar` format. Using a Macintosh and off-the-shelf software, these images were resized and colored, based on current scientific observations. Some interpretation and artistic license was taken to ensure that the planets would be photogenic. In most cases, the planets appear to be somewhat darker and duller in real life than they do in the final program.

CD–ROMs sourced from the National Space Science Data Center contained the data used for the Mars full planet views, Mars surface details, Venus surface details, and some moons. The data from these CD–ROMs has been worked on by NASA and JPL to remove gross distortions and to fill in missing data. The amount of data is so large and the images are so detailed that the surface data is divided into multiple files spanning several CD–ROMs for "ease of use."

Figure 6.23—Jupiter and one of its moons

These separate files are generally stored as sinusoidal equal-area projections. At this stage, it was determined which portions of each planet were needed, the files that corresponded to that portion were found, and custom Macintosh software was used to remap and seam them together at the appropriate resolutions. Other surface maps were generated by digitizing photographic prints and mapping and seaming them using special software.

Finally, these surface maps were transferred to SGI workstations where they were mapped onto planets for prechoreographed 3D moves. Ultimately, all of the surfaces of the 3D planets were created from flat (2D) maps.

Creating a Solar Eclipse

Existing eclipse material (both in film and High Definition video) was judged to be unusable for the piece in terms of action and framing. As a result, the solar eclipse effects were primarily created using a computer-controlled animation stand for movement. Using the preferred moving cutouts, it was possible to composite the proper color, stars, live sky, and hand painted elements in the best combination for a most realistic looking effect.

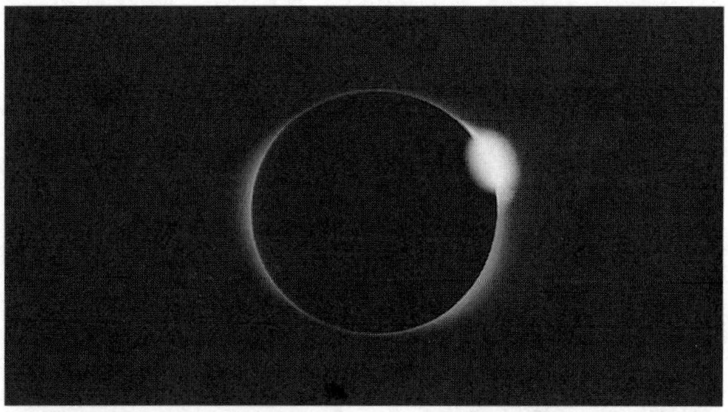

Figure 6.24—The solar eclipse

Getting It on Tape

Once all of the 3D renderings were completed, they were recorded to 1" digital High Definition videotape by transferring the still frames from the SGI workstations to a REBO ReStore-equipped Macintosh via Ethernet. The ReStore provides a 1920 by 1035 by 32-bit by 2 frame framebuffer with RGB video out. Custom software is used to display the images in the proper sequence as well as to control the High Definition VTR for single frame editing of the images to tape.

Integrating Live Action, CG, and Video

In the scenes that combine live action with the computer graphics, representative frames from the scenes in question were digitized from 1" digital tape using the Macintosh/ReStore combination and transferred to SGI workstations for position, perspective, lighting, and color matching.

In some cases, frames were retouched in the Macintosh (using Adobe Photoshop) so that seamless compositing could occur. The SGI workstations, running, in most cases, Wavefront software, generated alpha (key, or matte) channels so that objects could appear to pass in front of and behind corresponding live action elements. These key elements were transferred back to the Macintosh for the final edit. Both blue screen and luminance keyers were used in the edit room to create the final composites.

For the live action/miniature/computer graphics background frames, traditional blue screen and matting techniques were used. The only deviation from traditional techniques was the use of the Macintosh, Photoshop, and the ReStore to create "garbage" mattes.

In those live action shots where the computer monitor is visible, a Sony High Definition digital effects device was used to squeeze and transform the images into that monitor. The same effect could have been achieved by digitizing the live action footage and combining the CG elements in the computer and then single frame editing the composite back to High Definition tape. The real time DVE, while expensive, was less expensive in this case due to the length of the sequence involved.

In the close-ups of the computer monitor, the frame and backgrounds on the monitor were created on a Macintosh. In some cases, bluescreen from the "live" monitor was used for the image inserts, while in others hand drawn mattes were used. The images in these monitor shots were either rendered 3D computer graphics, frame-by-frame edited scenes from scientific data, or upconverted NTSC video. Images of the sun in soft X-rays from the Japanese Yohkoh satellite were transferred from 8mm Exabyte tapes to the Macintosh where they were sized, colored, and composited into the artist's rendering of the computer screen's frame. Mars and other computer graphics images were rendered the appropriate size for insertion into the screen. Material that was available only in

NTSC video format (the Saturn ring close-up and the Miranda flyover) was upconverted and appropriately positioned.

Figure 6.25—Using an HD DVE

Titles and Credits

Images for the credits were captured using a FOR–A digital High Definition still camera and retouched in the Macintosh/ReStore using Adobe Photoshop. Title text and credits were created on the Macintosh using Adobe Illustrator and rendered using Photoshop.

Figure 6.26—Title from The Astronomer's Dream

Comments from DP Neil Smith

> "*Astronomer's Dream,* for the kind of budget we had and the kind of film it was, was really two movies in one. One movie was the challenge in getting all of the digital data from the computer realm and turning it into High Definition pictures. At the same time, we were shooting a dramatic period piece with special effects, incorporating a miniature castle with a full size person—without real time digital video effects—keyed into a miniature landscape keyed over a fake sky.

"One of the nicest effects sequences in the piece dramatically illustrates the value of High Definition video for effects filmmaking. Creating the dream sequence where the planets start orbiting Kepler's head was actually very easy. First, the camera was locked off after being framed for the actor's position. Then the actor left the set, and we shot the scene without him, inserting a 4x8 blue card between the desk and the wall. Finally, we shot the scene with the actor in it. Having these two pieces made it easy to have the planets appear to orbit around his head and disappear as they passed behind him."

Figure 6.27—The planets circling Kepler

The Late Hybrid Era

Clearwater, Copper Canyon, and Dog Day in Manhattan

These three productions were the first produced in North America with the then brand new Panasonic portable UNIHI VTR and Betacam sized camera, and three of the first four productions using the equipment in the world. What was so important about these productions is that there really wasn't anything special about them.

For REBO engineers the main problems encountered were the ones that could reasonably be expected when learning to use entirely new equipment that had not yet been tested in the field. For the director and producer, the package made it possible to conceive shooting EFP-style productions in a way that would not be totally foreign to standard definition EFP video crews.

Clearwater: Celebrating the Hudson River

Clearwater: Celebrating the Hudson River (directed by Neil Smith; Chuck Clifton, DP) is a documentary on the revival of the Hudson River. Twenty years ago, the Hudson was dying a slow death because of pollution and public apathy. Today, the river is clean enough to drink from in many places, and most of this has been accomplished by the work of the Clearwater Society and its founder and spiritual leader, Pete Seeger.

Figure 6.28—Shooting the Clearwater from a chase boat

The project entailed two weeks of shipboard shooting on a 110-foot sailing sloop, helicopter shots, and a sequence shot aboard a canoe cruising the backwater tributaries of the Hudson River.

Figure 6.29—Engineering onboard the Clearwater

When this project was first proposed to coproduction partner NHK, it was conceived for shooting with 1" digital and studio UNIHI VTRs. In retrospect, it would have been extremely difficult if not impossible to get the project done this way, and many shots, especially the canoe shots, would never even have been suggested in the first place.

Figure 6.30—The prototype portable UNIHI on a canoe in the Hudson River

There were some difficulties convincing the representatives from Panasonic to okay the canoe shoot—after all, the package in use was still a prototype and was the only one of its kind in the world. Canoes are not reknowned for their stability and suitablity as camera platforms. Of course, there were no housings for the gear.

Figure 6.31—The view from the canoe

For the helicopter shots, having the portable package meant being able to go up in a small Bell helicopter, not a huge Sikorsky. A battery-powered downconverter provided the NTSC video feed for the pilot.

Figure 6.32—Helicopter mount

In addition to the field documentary aspect of the production, the final day of shooting included a live three-camera concert, shot in bitterly cold weather on a Manhattan pier. Two Sony HDC–300 cameras, one on a dolly, provided overall coverage. The Panasonic camera was on a Steadicam. All video footage was recorded on 1" digital VTRs, and to everyone's surprise and delight, the footage shot with the different cameras merged very well. There were differences, but they were minimal.

Figure 6.33—Panasonic AK–HC900 on a Steadicam

The reaction to the program in Japan and elsewhere was one of amazement that this type of production could be achieved in High Definition video; it just hadn't been possible before.

Copper Canyon

The next place the Panasonic portable package traveled was on safari driving through the mountainous Copper Canyon region of western Mexico. Given the remoteness of the location and the ruggedess of the terrain, this production (produced by Pat Weatherford, written and directed by Neil Smith; Chuck Clifton, DP/camera operator) would probably never have been proposed using studio UNIHI VTRs.

The camera was hand held from the front of a moving train and from the top of the equipment truck as the crew carefully negotiated winding mountain roads. Despite its newness and the hot and humid conditions encountered, the crew experienced only two major problems with the equipment—although one of them threatened the entire shoot very early on.

Figure 6.34—A handheld shot from the front of the train

At one point, the camera stopped working entirely. Fortunately, the manual was packed with the camera, but unfortunately, it was in Japanese. Working over a cellular phone hookup through a translator to an engineer in Japan, the engineer on the shoot was able to determine what part fizzled. Luckily, it was just a burnt out resistor, and it would be possible to fix the camera and continue the shoot. But there aren't many electronic parts shops in small towns in that part of Mexico. Eventually, a portable radio was taken apart and the necessary resistor was found, and the fix was made.

Later on, the camera was strapped to the wing of a single-engine plane. Downconverted video from the camera was viewable only on a 4" NTSC monitor. The relatively low quality of the downconverter and the small size of the monitor made it impossible to tell that there was a small problem, perhaps due to a faulty cable, and none of the footage could be used.

Dog Day in Manhattan

By the time *Dog Day in Manhattan* (directed by Neil Smith; Gabor Kover, DP/camera operator) rolled around, REBO engineers and crew had enough experience rigging the equipment for portability that it was possible to get a Steadicam shot where the camera operator is running down a Manhattan sidewalk.

Said Neil Smith, "It was like magic compared to where we came from."

New York: On The Edge

New York: On The Edge (*NYOTE*, series director Steven Dupler; directed by Steven Dupler, Alison Ellwood, Jacquie Ochs, and Marc Levin) is a traditional ENG-style field documentary coproduction with Tokyo Broadcasting System. Originally proposed as a thirteen-part series of fifteen-minute minidocumentaries, as of mid October, 1995, more than 20 episodes in the series were shot.

Topics covered in *NYOTE* include rave party culture; a Santeria ritual animal sacrifice; a satanic black mass presided over by the head of the East Coast Church of Satan; graffiti artists; an embalming class at the New York City Morgue; a group of illegal gun dealers displaying their wares in a Brooklyn housing project; homeless people living in shacks they built in the New York City subway system; transvestites and transsexuals; tattoing, piercing, and branding; and a private S&M club and public S&M performances.

Figure 6.35—Remains of a Santeria ritual from Believers

Production

Between six and ten hours of video are shot over the course of a two-day shooting schedule for each episode.

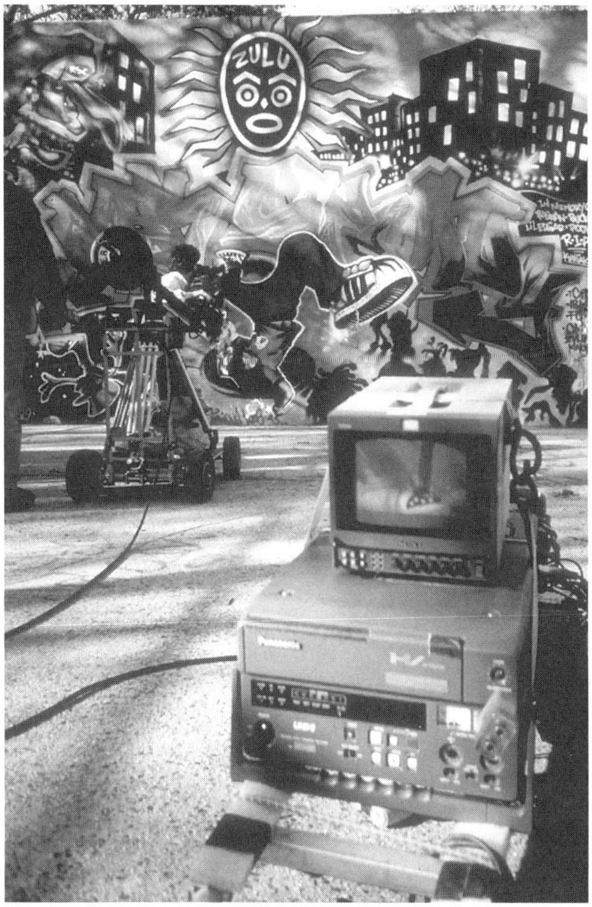

Figure 6.36—A typical NYOTE *engineering setup, from* Graffiti Wars

A typical crew for *NYOTE* consists of nine people: producer/director, line producer, engineer, camera operator, sound person, gaffer, grip, and two PAs. When the situation demands, armed security is hired.

When necessary, scenes are shot with a crew consisting of as few as four people: the director, engineer, camera operator, and sound person. This was the crew used for *Gunmen;* the script called for interviewing black market gun dealers in a small apartment in a New York housing project. The dealers arrived with two suitcases filled with fully loaded automatic weapons.

The location was an apartment building filled with nosy neighbors, so it was necessary to minimize the presence of the crew and the equipment. Furthermore, the gun dealers themselves were, predictably, a little skittish. The room where the interview took place was filled with eight gun dealers and their guns, and four crew: engineer, camera, director, and sound. A grip was positioned outside the apartment to act as a lookout, telling neighbors that scenes for a rap video were being taped.

NYOTE is shot with minimal additional lighting. The average lighting kit includes two or three battery-powered 1K lights with light boxes, a couple of flexible reflectors, some bounce cards, and a mixed roll of diffusion and color correction gel filters.

Power is always a big concern on *NYOTE* because of the need for mobility and working in odd locations. The entire package is rigged so that it can be run off batteries, and the equipment van is set up with an inverter, providing AC current so that batteries can be charged all along. See *Power* on page 53.

Some locations can be surprising. When shooting *Outside Society,* the episode on homeless people in New York, the script took the crew into the train tunnels under the city. There, many homeless have built themselves shacks, complete with electricity.

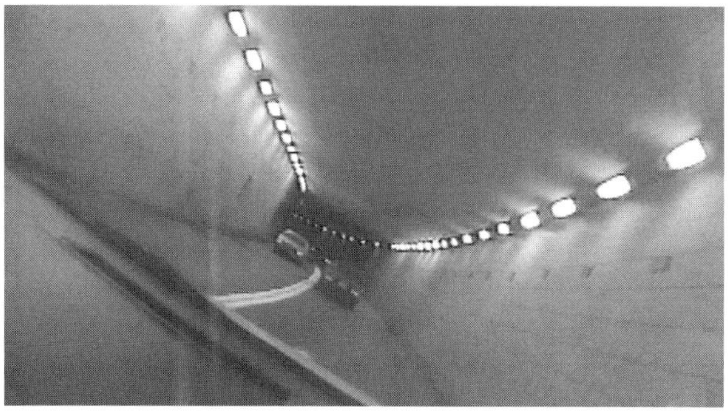

Figure 6.37—NTSC upconverted for Hackers

Prepared for a long day shooting in very low-light conditions, the crew found themselves able to use the AC they found there, after the engineer proclaimed it to be cleaner than the power that was in the studio.

Prior to the introduction of the Panasonic AU–HD1400 portable UNIHI, shooting High Definition meant being really buttoned up and inflexible. *NYOTE* has proven that it is possible to go out and shoot in the same fashion as an EFP crew, and be flexible enough and spontaneous enough to shoot virtually anywhere.

Figure 6.38—8 ball break from In the Pocket

Postproduction

Four days were scheduled for offline editing for each fifteen-minute episode on an Avid Media Composer. Because online editing, including subtitling, is being done in Japan, it was necessary to be very aware during the offline that the director and editor would not be in the online session to help resolve any problems that might arise. This meant that is was necessary to be very meticulous preparing the EDLs, recognizing that the editor might not be very proficient in written English. Consequently, considerably more time than usual was spent to clean the EDLs, and provide extensive notes on the desired audio mix.

NTSC footage that is shot is incorporated into the offline, and tapes are sent to Japan where they are upconverted. Framing decisions are left up to the online editors, providing them with some opportunity for contributing creatively to the program.

Woodstock '94: Live Multicamera Production Integrating High Definition Video and NTSC

This case study was originally written by C.R. Caillouet of Caillouet Technical Services and Charles Pantuso of HD VISION, Inc., and was revised and updated with their help for inclusion here. *For more of C.R.'s point of view, turn to* Charles R. Caillouet, Jr. *on page 114. Turn to* High Definition/Standard Definition Compatibility Issues *on page 62 for more from Charlie Pantuso.*

Multicamera High Definition production for live NTSC release is about five years old in North America. In 1991, *Sting: Live from the Hollywood Bowl* was the first live NTSC pay-per-view program shot using High Definition video equipment. In 1992, *Columbia Celebrates 30 Years of Bob Dylan* was also produced in High Definition and broadcast live to an international audience. On Saturday and Sunday, August 13th and 14th, 1994, Polygram Diversifed Entertainment and Woodstock Ventures turned the Winston Farm in Saugerties, New York into the site of *Woodstock '94* and added another event to the list of live multiformat productions.

Much has been written about the weather, crowd control, and access problems associated with the event. Less has been said about the technical innovations employed behind the stages to bring the live images home to millions of viewers. The people involved in the television production process are proud of the fact that an international team quietly integrated High Definition video with conventional television and multitrack audio technology into a live network origination facility. That facility delivered the high quality programming that the producers needed to fill the distribution pipeline described below. Very few problems arose in the production, and none of them were directly attributable to the High Definition equipment.

Woodstock '94's producers coordinated the television, audio, and radio production elements and released nearly 50 hours of concert programming over three days into various international broadcast media, including primary cable television, terrestrial broadcast television, pay-per-view cable television, and broadcast radio. Later, the concert footage would be edited for package distribution on audio compact disc, VHS videocassette, Hi–Vision satellite broadcast, and more cable television distribution. A documentary film was shot before and during the event for later theatrical release.

In order to preserve the musical performances at the maximum quality for future use, it was decided to record each stage performance in High Definition video. Polygram and production partner NHK (Nippon Hoso Kyokai—Japanese Public Broadcasting—the organization responsible for the development of 1125-line television) had teamed in the past to produce programming for both NTSC and Hi–Vision release so the capabilities of the technology were not foreign to them. However, *Woodstock '94* was the biggest and longest continuous broadcast in North America using the High Definition video/NTSC combination.

Polygram planned a documentary movie on the concert in conjunction with Propaganda Films and would have had to invest significant additional money to record a large portion of the 40-plus hours of performances from multiple angles on both the North and South Stage in film. The choice of High Definition video origination will enable the director to select portions of the 1125-line masters for transfer to film for the movie.

High Definition System Design

The High Definition video control rooms for each stage were functionally identical. The North Stage control room was built around a production console designed for *Columbia Celebrates 30 Years of Bob Dylan* at Madison Square Garden in 1992. The console contained a seven-input Sony production switcher (the largest currently available) with tally, a 30 x 20 RGB routing switcher, sync and video distribution for up to seven cameras and five recorders, and support for up to twelve 10" source monitors and three 18" program monitors.

Each stage was covered by seven cameras: two handheld cameras on stage, one dolly on track in front of the stage, one jib in front of stage right, two audience cameras in front of the mix tower (100 feet from the stage), and one audience right wide shot on a Condor lift (700 feet from the stage).

Five Sony HDD–1000 High Definition digital recorders recorded a switched program (two recorders were dedicated to the main program feed), a switched isolation feed (ISO), and two fixed ISO feeds from specific cameras.

Since 1990, the Sony HDC–300 Saticon (tube) camera has been the primary camera for most High Definition production. Since the *Dylan* concert in 1992, the Saticon cameras have been supplemented with Sony HDC–500 (CCD) cameras when available. It is now possible to fully equip a seven camera, five digital recorder unit with a mix of Saticon and CCD cameras from entirely within North America. However, long lenses and fiber-optic systems for long cable runs can still be limiting factors.

Conditions during the event were not conducive to operating with tube cameras, so additional CCD cameras were brought from Tokyo, and the Saticon cameras were limited to the more accessible, less critical "Condor" position at each stage. Most of the CCD cameras, and several digital recorders were shipped from Tokyo for this event.

Cable runs of up to 250 meters are practical under multicore cable control of the Sony Saticon and CCD cameras. Since there is no triaxial camera control system for current High Definition video cameras, runs over 250 meters call for fiber-optic control (to a maximum of 2000 meters.) The two fiber-optic control systems from NHK New York were used, and the remaining units were brought from Japan.

The choice for long lenses was the 40 x 15mm zoom with 2x extender, of which Canon and Fujinon had produced several. There was only one available for rental in North America, and the next longest available units were 10 x 12mm lenses from Nikon. Two of the Nikons were used for the jib cameras along with two more from Japan for the dolly cameras. Three 40 x 15mm and several older 22 x 18mm lenses were brought from Japan for the fixed cameras.

On the other end of the scale, handheld lenses are also a problem. At the time of *Woodstock '94*, there was only one lightweight Fujinon 6 x 12.5 lens available in North America, and two were brought from Japan. The fourth handheld was outfitted with a heavier Nikon 7 x 12 lens.

Audio System Design

Audio for each stage was handled by two independent multitrack recording units, alternating by performances, so that each one could be setting up for the next performance while the current performance was active. Prime and backup stereo feeds were brought to the High Definition control room from each audio unit, and a selection was made in order to keep the current audio on the main audio tracks and to provide proper monitor audio for the director. The eight digital tracks on the Sony HDD–1000 recorders enabled us to record prime audio from both units in case of a mistake in selection on the television board. Audio was also delivered directly to the NTSC integration truck where audio delays were added to match the video delay through the High Definition-to-NTSC converters, frame synchronizers, and NTSC digital effects units.

Voice communication (comm) was provided separately at both stages and in the integration unit. NTSC comm was extended to a producer at each stage control room to improve integration, but each stage produced continuously without regard for the output program. Integration did not have a serious impact on the High Definition production operations.

The NTSC integration unit also provided audio support for live talent at each stage to provide commentary and introduce acts for the pay-per-view audience.

Construction

The sheer magnitude of the event placed huge loads on the construction crews, and the television crews were forced to wait in line for trailer placement, platform construction, and heavy equipment. Preparation took seven days from initial equipment arrival to shoot date including one day for construction, one day for physical assembly, four days for external and internal cabling, and one day for testing and integration.

The trailer positioning, leveling, and physical installation of equipment took longer than predicted, especially at the South Stage site. Power distribution became a problem because of the difficulty of finding enough hardware to support such a big operation.

Hanging fiber between the stages also took more time than planned and had an impact on our communication ability because the phones followed that path. Walkie-talkies and cell phones were used extensively.

The difficulty of scheduling use of a large equipment package and the complexity of shipping it though customs required a lot of support from NHK Tokyo. Equipment already in the U.S. for World Cup Soccer, as well as two shipments from Tokyo as equipment became available, required us to stagger the installation schedule to accommodate shipping.

After the event, cleanup became a pressing issue. The field was so muddy and rank that it was declared a health hazard area and special protective equipment was required for the cleanup crews. The fiber and camera cable running through the mud had to be thoroughly cleaned and dried prior to packing and the process took most of a day.

NTSC Integration

In October 1991, the first North American NTSC pay-per-view broadcast from High Definition origination was delivered. The *Sting* concert was produced completely in High Definition video and converted to NTSC for distribution.

In October 1992, seven high definition cameras with four NTSC cameras in two production switchers were used to produce another live NTSC pay-per-view event. Graphics and replays were added in NTSC. The director of the *Dylan* concert was forced to think in terms of two programs, and there was much concern about the integrity of the High Definition video program on tape because of the availability of additional cameras in NTSC for the live program. This approach was chosen because of the limitations on the size of the High Definition production switcher and the number of cameras available.

In August 1994, *Woodstock '94* represented another step forward in the development of the role of high definition with NTSC television in live events. It provided an opportunity to test a new way of integrating the two media. The stage production was essentially divorced from the program integration operation by "joining in progress" whichever performance was appropriate at the time. This operation was much the same as a local station with a live announcer "cherry picking" live feeds from a number of networks. This approach obviously would not always work, but it provided a feel for the multistage character of *Woodstock '94*.

The High Definition production operation at each stage was relatively straightforward and not particularly unusual compared with other productions. There were fewer cameras than a typical NTSC event, and the director had better quality images than would have been available in a video assisted film shoot. The most significant aspect of this event was in the combination of High Definition video technology with conventional NTSC production services.

As was mentioned earlier, five Sony HDD–1000 High Definition digital VTRs recorded the switched program and several ISO feeds. To feed the NTSC integration unit, two high quality converters provided prime and backup NTSC program feeds and four medium quality converters provided NTSC versions of the ISO feeds for offline recording and feeds to the video image magnification (IMAG) video screens adjacent to the stage.

A large concert venue with IMAG presents additional requirements to a High Definition video production that would be trivial in an NTSC production. IMAG is often controlled from a different production site than the main production. The IMAG director may take feeds from the program production, may add additional cameras, or may combine the two. It was not practical to operate additional cameras at Woodstock '94 because of cost, access problems, and the duration of the event, so additional converters were provided for IMAG use of the High Definition cameras.

The main High Definition video router at each stage provided each IMAG director with a router bus into a dedicated converter. The output of the program converter and the dedicated ISO camera converters at each stage were also available as IMAG sources.

Dealing with the Difference in Aspect Ratios

One issue that always comes up in High Definition video productions with strong NTSC participation is the difference in aspect ratio. Pay-per-view promoters usually avoid the issue until late in the planning cycle and then object to the simplest solution: letterboxing. Letterboxing delivers the entire 1.78:1 area of the High Definition image but leaves black bars at the top and bottom of the 1.33:1 NTSC image area.

There seems to be a common fear in the pay-per-view world that viewers will demand money back on the grounds of "technical problems" if they see black bands. This usually leads to a decision to air the live event in "edge crop" where the sides of the widescreen image are discarded in the conversion process. Of course, the users of the High Definition video program are, understandably, concerned that the director will focus his attention on the 1.33:1 area and not use the widescreen advantage. That usually leads to concerns over how the person switching the selectable ISO will cover the event for postproduction.

For *Woodstock '94*, a settlement was negotiated that not only quieted the above concerns, but enabled the pay-per-view broadcasters to test the market in nonprime time and gave the viewers a way of identifying live and delayed broadcasts. The live broadcasts were converted using a compromise (letterbox/crop) 1.56:1 aspect ratio which hid a smaller black border on the top and bottom in the overscan area on most receivers and discarded less of the picture area than would 1.33:1.

The backup converters ran in letterbox mode and the NTSC D–2 recordings for *Woodstock Overnight* were made from these signals. The *Overnight* replays were made over a stylized background that made the top and bottom area seem to be part of the program, much the same as the sports ticker on *CNN Headline News*. This turned what was perceived as a drawback of the widescreen format into an advantage. The promoters seemed happy with this approach and even agreed not to complain if a switch to the letterbox mode was required in the live broadcast because of equipment failure.

The scope of the event caused another problem. Over 200 hours of material would need to be converted to NTSC offline tapes for the film editors and video editors to select cuts for the after-market products. The estimated time to provide those tapes was considerable, so Polygram asked for additional converters to make NTSC copies of the ISO sources. The NTSC unit recorded a common "quad-split" offline tape for scene selection after the event and before the conversions were complete. This also would reduce the cost of High Definition-to-film conversions for the movie.

Graphics and Digital Video Effects

The conventional NTSC mobile unit provided most of the available bells and whistles for packaging the program, including digital effects, still store, and live graphics. Used this way, the hybrid approach can actually simplify both operations and make it more practical to originate in High Definition video by moving the bells and whistles items to the NTSC domain.

Equipment Reliability

August can be a fun time in North America: hours of 90+ degrees, sunshine, and then pouring rain. The crane cameras provided an overview of the crowds that was at times overwhelming. The sea of mud, tents, lawn chairs, and wet people was amazing. It was quite a test of equipment reliability.

The air conditioners were well used, both to remove the heat and as dehumidifiers when the rains came. The environment in the control rooms was not too bad, and although dirt generally reduces the life of tape heads, no immediate effects of the dirty environment were apparent.

The rain was an annoyance but had no direct impact on any equipment. The mud actually caused more problems than the rain. The cameras all fared well with one exception. At different times, both stages were subjected to rowdy mud throwing crowds at the front of the stage. The cameras were pretty well protected so recovery usually consisted of taking the camera out of service and cleaning the front of its lens. One of the less responsible musical groups convinced the crowds to throw mass quantities of mud at the stage, to the point where the entire stage—including the dolly—had to be washed down before the concert could continue. Somewhere in the washing process, a ground fault took down a camera head. It was replaced with a spare and the show went on.

Crew Requirements

The television and audio production crew totaled over 220 people of which about 30 were specific to High Definition. At least half of the High Definition crew would have been required if the stage performances had been shot only in NTSC, and a large concert event might have required more support personnel than this one. These event-specific variables make the estimation of the personnel overhead for using High Definition video in the production virtually impossible. However, it is safe to conclude that, because the producers will be able to use the High Definition video to make the film, actual personnel requirements were certainly lower than they would have been if separate film crews were also shooting the event.

Chapter 7

Creative Considerations

John Alonzo

John Alonzo shot his first feature picture, Bloody Mama *starring Shelley Winters, Robert DeNiro, and Bruce Dern for Roger Corman in 1969. Prior to that he was a documentary cameraman for National Geographic. Among his best known films are* Chinatown, Norma Rae, Scarface, Steel Magnolias, *and* Star Trek: Generations. World War II: When Lions Roared, *a four-hour miniseries for NBC, was his first feature-length HDTV project.*

On His First Experience Shooting High Definition Video

"It wasn't until 1993 that I got my first opportunity to shoot in High Definition because nobody talked to me about it before then. It's not that I'm anti-progress or anti-new toys. I love new toys, and if a new gizmo can help me make a better picture, then I'll use it. In my opinion, Panavision makes the best cameras in the world right now. But if somebody comes along with a better one, I'll try it. The same thing with film. I have a loyalty to Eastman Kodak, but one day a story came along and a Fuji stock was more appropriate for the look I wanted. So it made a lot of sense to use it.

"The first thing I actually did in High Definition was test the Sony HDC–500 right after it came to the United States. I went down to Epcot Center and met with some people from Disney's production company and Sony.

"They said to me, 'The camera is yours. Do anything you want with it.' And I asked them to tell me about it. One of the interesting things that they told me was that the camera could be rated, in film terms, at 400, 500, 800, 1000, even 2000.

"I went out to join the crew from Disney, and I looked at the High Definition monitor they had and I said, 'My God. This is wonderful.' But everything they were shooting was perfectly lit in bright sunlight. When they were finished with it, I kept the camera and some of the crew members wanted to stay with me and we ended up shooting until three in the morning—available light all around Epcot. We pushed the camera all the way to what they called 2000 ASA. I kept asking the engineer to do stuff that he didn't know if it would work. He'd say, 'Well, I don't know what you're talking about, but let's try it.' I remember asking him if we could do a shutter speed change during a pan. The idea was to start a shot pointing inside a brightly lighted interior and pan the camera, and I told him, 'As the camera pans to the exterior you're going to lose the light, so you'll have to gradually change the shutter speed. Can you do that?'

"In the end, after a couple of rehearsals, we got this wonderful transition from what was basically, in film exposure terms, an f4.5 for the interior shot to an f1.4 outside to an f2.8 to an f2 as we panned around outside—and you just cannot see it. It was having like an automatic iris, but you couldn't see it adjust. I fell in love with the camera because you just can't do that in film. You do have a shutter on film cameras but it isn't capable of such subtleties as the 500 is."

On Approaching a Project: How High Definition Is Different from Film

"One major thing you have to rethink are your lighting requirements. The lighting requirements for High Definition are in some cases quite different from film or traditional video. But there aren't really any major changes.

"In many cases you can use instruments that aren't as strong. You do still have a balancing problem if you're going to do an interior/exterior shot. But, the DP wouldn't have to overlight the interior a lot in order to balance the background (for example, through a window) in order to see detail. The electronics the engineer has can also help the DP. The engineer can fiddle with the dials and move the highlight down just a bit. You can't do that on film. The only option is to put enough light on (the subject in the interior) to balance the outside.

"I got a lot of experience lighting High Definition working on a four-hour miniseries NBC called *World War II: When Lions Roared.* It had to be lighted for television, but if I had been lighting it for film which for transfer to video it would have been a different look. As it was, we were able to get away with some so-called film lighting techniques. For one thing, it wasn't necessary to use those enormous instruments that you have to use for film. We were able to use a 10k for sunlight and it was perfect. On film, It would have been necessary to use 12k HMIs to give us the hard sunlight look we needed.

"There's a bluescreen shot in *WWII* where Roosevelt and Churchill meet aboard a ship. It's supposed to be bright sunlight, so we hung one 10K about fifteen or twenty feet up in the air and let that be the sun. It cast only one shadow, and the bounce off the floor of the set was enough to give us this feel that you were outside. We put a silk on the left side behind the camera and threw some 2Ks and 4Ks into the silk and that gave us the sort of wraparound ambient light that God does. For film, that probably would have been two 12K HMIs, through a silk, and you still would have got a double shadow, or you would have had to shoot it wide open. And you would be guessing on film until you saw it—the next day at the earliest. With High Definition and with the engineer's help, we were able to manipulate the image on the set until we just blew out the sunlight and it looked terrific.

"As far as crew requirements go, it's pretty much the same shooting High Definition as for film. Except for the working relationship between the director, the DP, and the chief engineer, the rest of it is the standard crew. On a film, a DP would have a first and second assistant, a camera operator, myself, a gaffer, and a grip. When you do it in HD it's the same number of people except, maybe one more because you want to add a tape operator, and the job responsibilities change a little bit—one of the camera assistants is replaced by the engineer. So, with respect to cost—it's about the same because there are savings in time and lighting.

"Shooting in High Definition can be a lot more efficient than shooting in film, depending on the working styles of the Director and DP. That's because there is less guesswork on camera moves and staging because the director can see it right there in the monitor and say, 'Okay, that works, let's do it that way.' In film the director has to look through the lens, and then do a rehearsal, and look at the video assist, and try it. And then they'll try different ways because they're not sure of it. They don't have this High Definition monitor on the set that says, 'This is what you're going to get.' With video assist you can't really tell what you're going to get. And people are already criticizing the lighting on these little color monitors that are not perfect. The video assist cameras are not perfect, you don't get a good enough image to make critical judgments. Shooting High Definition removes a lot of the guesswork of film.

"Lenses are still a problem for me. I would like to have a larger variety of lenses so the camera could be made more compact and more portable.

"Aside from that, the director and DP have to recognize that they've taken on a big responsibility because what they are seeing on the High Definition monitor is what they are going to get. You no longer have the excuse, 'The lab will fix it,' or 'Don't worry about it, I can light it dark.' Now you have to prove that you know what you're doing lightingwise as a cameraman because there's this beautiful monitor saying, 'Is that what we're going to get?' 'Yeah, that's what we're going to get.'"

On the Importance of Communication

"Establishing a tight working relationship with the engineer and technical crew on a High Definition shoot is an absolute prerequisite, the top priority.

"From the first time I shot some commercials on conventional video the biggest hurdle for me was communicating with that engineer from an aesthetic viewpoint, not a technical one. I found myself talking to the engineer and saying, 'Look, I know that you have your peaks, pedestal, and gain and all of that, but I want you to think about the fact that creatively, it needs to look a certain way, and you should respect that. We want it to look overexposed, grainy, or noisy. So, can you just give us that look?' And it offends them. As it should, it would offend me to shoot something in a way that I didn't agree with.

"Until I started working in High Definition, I'd never really had a good working relationship and camaraderie with the video engineers. They're just as much artists as I am.

"A big hurdle film DPs have to jump over is to learn to communicate with the High Definition video engineers. When I was asked to shoot *World War II: When Lions Roared,* my first move when I got on location was to meet with the High Definition crew engineering the production. I sat down with them and said, 'I'm going to shoot this production like I would film. This *is* film as far as I'm concerned. If I step over a boundary, don't say 'No' to me, instead say, 'Come here and let me show you why.' In other words, explain your reasoning to me. Is it something technical and the signal won't be suitable for broadcast? Or, is it something that's not to your liking? I may say, 'I don't care, it's to my liking.' But don't be negative about it.

"We (C.R. Caillouet, the chief engineer on *WWII,* and I) hit it off beautifully, and as a result, working with CR was like having a color timer on the set with me. Which, I can tell you, was wonderful. Another member of the engineering crew (Jimmy Lucas) was like having a perfect assistant DP in the truck really seeing the image clearly without any ambient light, and really listening to the sound and so on. The whole thing was like having the lab and other postproduction trades right there on the set to make sure that everything was okay as we went along.

"Again, the stumbling block is getting the engineering world to communicate with the production people, the aesthetic people—on their terms."

On Transferring High Definition Video to Film

"When you shoot a film, the first thing you do is test the material—the stock you want to use, and the talent. If you have a particular leading lady, you test her and you see what kind of lighting she goes through, the same with leading men. I was the DP on *Star Trek: Generations* and I tested every single actor in that picture in various lighting situations. It not only helps their egos, it also helps me. The tests were sent to the lab and I would go to the lab and say, 'Patrick Stewart shouldn't look that pale, I want him to have more warmth.' So we'd correct the color. The color timers would get those notes so that when we were shooting the movie, they had those guidelines to work with. But even after we started shooting the movie, every morning I'd talk to the lab and ask, 'What are my printer lights? How do things look?' And so on? You can imagine the anxiety of having to wait to get the material back. You can imagine the anxiety of depending on somebody else's judgment of what is right and what is wrong as far as the look of the film is concerned. Having the engineer on the set can really reduce these anxieties.

"High Definition transferred to film via the EBR (electron beam recorder) process is gorgeous. And, it can be anything you need it to be. You can take a scene shot in High Definition, go through the EBR and fiddle with the image as it is transferred. You can print it on (Eastman 52) 45 negative stock or on Fuji stock if you want to, and go through another creative step and end up with exactly the look the project calls for, and by the time the audience sees it projected they'll think it was shot with some brand new film because it will have an entirely different look.

"I can't do that with film. But I can sit there in front of a screen before it goes to the EBR and say to the technician, 'Okay, take that blue down a little bit more. But leave the skin tones alone.' And they can. Or I might ask, 'Blacken those shadows down, I don't want to see anything back there. But leave the skin tones alone.' The look can be manipulated before the transfer. It's like being in an optical house without having to make three layers like you could using the old imbibition (IB) process. The last pictures made using the IB process were *Chinatown* and the first of the *Godfather* movies. The reason the IB process was so wonderful was that by making separate color matrices you could manipulate colors individually and have more control over the final look. And then they did away with the IB. So we're stuck now, we can't do it any more. But the EBR provides us with this same capability and it's wonderful to be able to have it again."

On Shooting 16:9

"I would say to all video camera operators and video directors that shooting High Definition is not television; a High Definition camera is not like a Betacam camera. It's also not a Panavision camera. High Definition is another tool, another toy, another way to shoot drama, comedy, or action. It has the advantage of film in the scope of wideness of the screen. It has an advantage over film in that it has far more depth of field. It has an advantage over video because you can now light with far more subtlety than you can with NTSC. A piece of white card can be enough to light the front of somebody's face.

"I think that television has ruined audiences' taste in the visual sense because everything is a close-up. Everything is talking heads. Some stories can take this approach, while other stories can't because the visual impact does not advance the story. The 16:9 format of High Definition presents wonderful possibilities for directors used to working in 4:3. You can now shoot a big close-up and not have to center the actor up in the screen; you can put them off to the side.

"The challenge for video camera operators is not to do what they are used to doing in NTSC and instinctively zoom into tight close-up. Instead, you can afford to be a little more generous, and give the audience a reference point as to where they are.

"Actors and directors are also influenced by the shape of the television screen. When we started shooting *Star Trek: Generations* using the actors from the *Star Trek: The Next Generation* television series, I noticed that the actors were leaning very close together, unconsciously, when they were in a two-shot. That comes from years of having to do that for television. I had to go over there and separate them. Finally, they fell in love with the idea of being able to talk to an actor that's more than eighteen inches away. It's unnatural to talk to someone that close all the time. It's unnatural to perform that way.

"I like the 16:9 format of High Definition video. It's closer (than NTSC is) to what a lot of cinematographers want, which is 2:1. 16:9 still gives me, as an artist, the canvas that I like. And, if I understand correctly, you can extract anything you want out of 16:9 if you're going to release on film."

On Shooting with the Sony HDC–500 Camera

"I like the Sony HDC–500 camera very much. I just wish they had a series of lenses that were more movie-friendly. The 500 has this 10:1 zoom which is a huge piece of glass, and this makes it inconvenient sometimes to move the camera around and put it in tight spaces. You can put a follow focus at the camera, just like a Panavision camera, and you can also move the finder from the top of the camera to the side, which more film camera operators are used to.

"One of the complaints people have shooting with the 500 is that there is always an umbilical cord connecting the camera to the VTR. That's silly. Movie cameras always have cables now. There's a video assist cord at least, and who knows what else gets put on it?

"I wouldn't change anything about the camera, but it would be great to have a recorder that is capable of recording what the camera is really seeing. The camera is actually capturing more information than the recorder (the HDD–1000) can record. My philosophy is, 'You should give artists Rolls Royces and accept that sometimes they might make Chevys out of them. But don't give them Chevys to start with.'

"You have to have the best of everything to work with. We do it all the time in the movies. I get the sharpest lenses from Panavision, and I screw them up by putting filters in front of them and diffusing them and shooting them wide open, but that's artistic taste. It has nothing to do with hating the technology; we all want all the best that technology can give us.

"Panavision has always been baffled by the fact that DPs don't use the lenses to their full capacity. They would rather see it sharp, crisp, clear with depth of field from here to Pomona. But sometimes the story just doesn't call for it."

Final Impressions

"What I love about shooting in the digital format—I don't like calling it video—is, to use the cliché, instant gratification. Working in High Definition is an immediate thing, and it became better as the rapport grew between myself and CR. We had a terrific time in Prague. CR would come over to me and say, 'Come here and take a look at this. Is this what you want?' And I'd look at it and say, 'Yeah. That's what I want. Are you questioning it?' He might say, 'Well, it just seems a little bright to me, John, it just seems like it's too full.' And I'd say, 'All right, play with it.' And he'd play with the image, and he'd bring it down to a different level, and I'd say, 'That's kind of nice. Let me do something else.' Maybe I'd go and turn off some lights. 'Now how does it look?' And I'd go look at it, and say, 'Oh, that's perfect. Let's leave it like that.' It was nice. It's a kind of collaboration that you don't have when you're shooting film."

Charles R. Caillouet, Jr.

After graduating from Louisiana State University, where he studied Electrical Engineering, C.R. worked in broadcast stations in Louisiana before moving to Texas to become a contract project engineer for NASA. There, he learned about audio systems, computers, and digital video, and built television systems to go in places people couldn't. C.R., through his company Vision Unlimited, has provided engineering services for dozens of High Definition video productions—projects as diverse as World Cup Soccer, space shuttle launches for NASA, and Woodstock '94.

On Making the Transition from NTSC to High Definition Video

"The most difficult part of embarking on the production of any new live event, especially if the crew has never worked with High Definition video before, is communicating with the producers, directors, and camera operators and helping them understand how to use High Definition video to the best advantage.

"Even producers with experience in both High Definition video and NTSC sometimes overlook an important issue in an integrated High Definition/NTSC production. The prevailing reason for getting involved in coproducing an integrated production is that, for marginal additional cost, it is possible to have a high quality program in the archive for future use. What they don't fully realize is that they need to think about more than one product throughout the process.

"One implication is that the director is often focused on creating a product strictly from an NTSC perspective. This causes the director to think only about formatting the program to fit into a 4:3 format, ignoring 16:9, and to think solely in terms of how the program will look on the small screen, not on a big screen. This often results in an ineffective use of High Definition's wider aspect ratio, rapid cutting between shots, and not taking advantage of the extra detail that the format can capture. And with good reason, because the director is only thinking about creating an NTSC product.

"The director goes into the production thinking 'How can I use this tool (High Definition video) to do my job, which is to make an NTSC program?' On the other hand, an experienced High Definition producer approaches the problem by asking 'How can I get the NTSC people to shoot a High Definition show?'

"Where the problem normally surfaces is when making the decision about how the program will be broadcast. Will it be in letterbox or in edge crop? Producers find out that the down-converters can convert to either format, so they wait to decide until the last moment. And this is very late in the process to be making such an important decision.

"Another place where the aspect ratio can really be a problem is answering the question 'Who's going to switch the ISO recording?' Whichever 'side' controls the switched ISO covers their butts for postproduction. Often the answer is to create two ISO feeds, one for the NTSC director, one for the High Definition production.

"It's important to think about these issues early on during preproduction. The director and camera operators will need to get used to framing their shots differently, sometimes not coming quite as tight on close-ups. The director may need to slow down the pace of cutting and take advantage of what the High Definition video format offers. (Remember the separate NTSC switched ISO reel? A delayed broadcast show may have time to be reedited for NTSC to speed things up.)

See *Woodstock '94: Live Multicamera Production Integrating High Definition Video and NTSC* beginning on page 100 for more discussion about integrating High Definition video and NTSC.

On Shooting HD for Film

"Much has been said about using High Definition video for the big screen. One thing that people tend to forget is that most film is projected at 24 fps and not the 30 fps of HDTV. This means that you can actually see more on the HDTV monitor that you can on the screen because of problems in the temporal conversion from 30 fps to 24 fps. It's not that there's a problem in the conversion process, it's that the end result is going to be projected at 24 fps.

"So, when you're shooting High Definition video for film, you need to think in terms of film projection. For example, cinematographers know that they can pan only so fast before the image starts to judder. In both High Definition video and NTSC, there isn't the same problem. This is an issue which the average video camera operator never has to deal with, so they will pan fast—because they can. However, in the process of converting the 30 fps High Definition video to 24 fps film, the 'picket fence' problem can crop up if you're not careful to follow some film rules.

"Because the image on the High Definition video monitor is so good and plays back the same way, there is a tendency to think of it as WYSIWYG (What You See Is What You Get). But this may not be true in the temporal domain when transferring the High Definition video original to film for distribution."

On the Future of High Definition Video

"As integrated High Definition video/NTSC productions become more common, it would be very helpful if the NTSC and High Definition video equipment could both be operated at the NTSC vertical rate. The ability to operate High Definition video equipment at both 59.94 fields/second and 60.00 fields/second vertical rates would eliminate most of the NTSC frame-rate conversion problems. I think that the manufacturers should provide modifications for existing equipment to support either rate.

"The presence of both 59.94 and 60.00 fields/second compatibility would make the transition to High Definition video production and broadcasting less stressful, and less expensive. Production expenses would be reduced because it would be easier to mix High Definition and NTSC equipment when appropriate. The Grand Alliance has recognized this need and has included both frame rates in the proposed ATV transmission standard, although it is not clear whether production equipment manufacturers will officially endorse the concept and support it in the marketplace.

"There is also a need for integration of digital audio among High Definition video, NTSC, and multitrack facilities without complex standards converters. The next generation of High Definition video recorders should allow for 48.000 KHz audio rates at 59.94 fields/second, making possible live NTSC conversion with integral frames and direct digital audio transfer. The conversion should take place in the recorders to guarantee exchange of standard tapes.

"High quality, widescreen, live production for multiple release formats is alive and well and the next few years will prove to be very interesting.

"However, as we move from where we are now into the near future, the question will not necessarily be 'How much do we produce for High Definition transmission?' but 'How much do we produce for 16:9 standard resolution?' It's not clear that we'll have much delivery of High Definition programming in North America in the next few years: Broadcasters want lots of '525' channels. This means that things could be headed in the direction of more integrated High Definition/standard definition productions, not fewer. The standard definition products might be widescreen component instead of NTSC, but many of the issues would be the same."

Randall Dark

Randall is the founder, president, and CEO of HD VISION, a High Definition production, postproduction, and creative facility located near Dallas, Texas. Since his first High Definition production in 1987, Randall has been personally involved in over 120 projects, over 60 of them since HD VISION opened in March, 1993. HD VISION is the second company in the world to broadcast regularly scheduled programming in High Definition video, originating more than a dozen broadcasts in HD-BMAC from their offices in Irving, TX via satellite to college campuses in the northern United States in September and October, 1994. Randall has a BA and Honors BA in Theater from the University of Ottawa.

On the Increasing Acceptance of High Definition

"I got my start in HDTV production in 1987 in Canada working with John Galt and Charles Pantuso on *Chasing Rainbows* for the CBC, the first miniseries shot on High Definition in North America—if not the world.

"Since starting HD VISION in early 1993, I've noticed a whole new interest in High Definition production that I believe is directly attributable to several factors:

1 The availability of new and inexpensive—especially considering the image quality—High Definition cameras and VTRs.

2 An increasing number of venues to exhibit programming originated in High Definition video.

3 The availability of a very affordable new semiconductor technology that will revolutionize video projection and flat panel displays for computers and video.

4 More and more producers are grasping the fact that widescreen is the future and originating now in widescreen is a very smart bet against the future.

5 The FCC is close to selecting a transmission standard for High Definition, and contrary to what others believe, there will be regularly scheduled High Definition transmission in the United States—actually narrowcasting via satellite—by September, 1996.

"Another reason that the acceptance of High Definition has been delayed is that people have been spoiled by NTSC. In NTSC, you're looking at a technology that has evolved pretty much to its fullest extent both as far as quality and portability is concerned.

"But if you really want portability you shoot with Betacam. If you want quality, you shoot in 35mm, or in High Definition, which is faster than shooting with film. With an experienced High Definition crew, I have found that the amount of time required for setup, blocking, and lighting is reduced because of the immediacy and interactivity afforded by the electronic image. This is especially true for bluescreen work. The director, DP, and key crew members can see the product as they create it, and can communicate what they require for a shot more clearly and more quickly.

"Also, High Definition VTRs basically have no load time (loads are 63 minutes in length), which means that momentum can be maintained during the shoot day; there is no need to stop and load a new roll of film. Also 'safety' takes are almost never required because in most instances the take can be reviewed instantly on set to determine its suitability.

"The very portability and quality of NTSC means that it doesn't force you to think about what you're doing. You can literally just point and shoot. For some applications that's okay and very desirable, for others its not. Sometimes the quality of what appears on the screen suffers because no one is forced to think hard about what they're doing."

On Making the Transition

"From my experience, most of the multicamera directors I have worked with have come from the NTSC video world. The biggest problem—and the biggest opportunity—working with them is getting them to use the 16:9 High Definition frame effectively.

"The directors and camera operators really get jazzed when they realize what they can do with this new aspect ratio. There's much more to play with. Plus High Definition images contain a lot more texture and a lot more detail. This is positive if the only product is for widescreen release or you can convince the producers to release the program letterboxed.

"The problems arise when the program will be released in multiple formats and aspect ratios. Then the director and camera operators, who have just had their vision expanded, have to force themselves to remember to protect for the 4:3 frame they've just left behind. This is much easier to do in sports than it is for concerts and dramatic programs.

"The next time you watch a football game, imagine that there are another couple of inches of screen on either side of the one you're watching. Imagine what you'd see there. There's more action, you're going to see approaching tackles a little earlier. Barry Sanders is an incredible running back and his ability to anticipate is amazing. Often he starts moving before we can see his opponents enter the frame. He can see them, but we can't. With widescreen, we will see more action, but it's still quite easy to protect for 4:3. If you look at virtually all sports this rule applies.

"This is not true for concerts and dramatic programs. There are compromises in framing, pacing, and shot selection that the director and camera operators have to make that, in the short term, distract from the ability to create purely for the 16:9 frame. A shot that is beautifully framed in 16:9 can be disastrous in 4:3. Although the director might be drawn to a close two-shot in 16:9, in a 4:3 crop that same shot will cut off portions of the picture unacceptably. Protecting safe action in two different aspect ratios at the same time is challenging but possible. The compromises that must be made are minor when compared with the benefits the format provides.

"When my company works with clients and directors who are new to the format, we feel that it is part of our job to let them know about the possibilities and potential complications the format offers them in their particular application. But we've tried very hard to create a world that is as much like what they are used to having in NTSC as possible. When they walk into one of our trucks, the only real difference is they're looking at monitors that are 16:9 and high resolution, and not that other format.

"There *is* a learning curve to High Definition. There is with any new technology. But High Definition is not a limiting technology, it's an enhancing technology. High Definition provides creatives with a wide variety of tools to work with, and I've seen moderately talented people be successful producing in High Definition because the pictures—all by themselves—are so spectacular."

Final Impressions

"I was trained as a writer and director in the theater, so I don't have a formal education in film or video. Among other things, this means I don't have a bias towards either medium.

"I attended the 1995 Jackson Hole Wildlife Film Festival and I though to myself, 'Why are people still using film to document wildlife?' Film romanticizes everything, we all know that anything on film is history. I know why they don't use conventional video—it's so low res. High Definition is a perfect alternative. It has enough color and physical resolution to 'document' the world without giving it the romantic, historical look and feel that film does.

"After more than a decade of production, the biggest drawback and problem of High Definition is that not enough really talented people have had the opportunity to shoot with it. HD Vision is set up the way it is because I want to get this technology in the hands of everyone who wants to use it.

"It is now possible to rent a JVC High Definition camera/JVC W-VHS VTR package for about $900/day. Anyone who is a competent video or film camera operator should be able to achieve very good results using this package, which is suitable for ENG-type shooting, though it's still not as portable as a Betacam camcorder. This package was used to shoot the NBA *Stay in School Jam* which was edited for use during the half time show for the 1994 NBA *All-Star Game* (see *Philip Hack, On the 1995 NBA All-Star Game* beginning on page 123). This package was also used for the 50th Anniversary of the United Nations. This marked the first time we were able to go to a standard NTSC video rental house, rent a lens (a 60:1), and use it.

"From the growth of my own company, I know that the use of High Definition video is growing. More importantly, much of the work we do is for consumption here in the United States, with only about 25% of our business produced primarily for domestic consumption in Japan. About 25% of the High Definition video production we do is aired on conventional television here in the United States, projects like *Woodstock '94,* and the rest is for presentation in High Definition for special music and sporting events, corporate presentations and product launches, film-style documentary production, and for location based entertainment uses including ride films."

Steven Dupler

Steven is VP of Development for REBO Entertainment. He has been with REBO since 1989. Prior to joining REBO he was a reporter for the New York Post *and was a Senior Editor for* Billboard *magazine where he covered technology and music television.*

On Producing and Directing *New York: On The Edge*

"My background is as a reporter and print journalist, so I feel that it's important to speak primarily as a storyteller, then as a director.

"The most important thing about producing and directing a documentary series like *New York: On The Edge* (*NYOTE*) is telling a story. Fifteen minutes is a very short period of time to tell a story that's captivating, and the key to these stories working is twofold:

1 Finding really strong characters and letting them develop themselves—this is a *cinema verite* series and it has to be the characters' own words.

2 Taking advantage of the aspect ratio of High Definition video and to approach things in a more cinematic fashion.

"I like shooting in High Definition video because of all of the reasons that people generally cite—things like the widescreen aspect ratio, color fidelity, image clarity, etc., and I think all of these things can really enhance telling that story. But, I think we've also proven with *NYOTE* that there is a place within High Definition production for all types of imaging media—8mm film, 16mm film, Hi-8 video, and

Betacam to name just a few—to add their particular look and value and be blended together.

"As a producer and director I've never felt hampered either by the High Definition equipment or the process, but this may be that my only experience producing and directing has been in High Definition video—it's all I've known.

"I feel that we were really fortunate to make this series with Tokyo Broadcasting System (TBS), because of all of the Japanese networks involved in High Definition production and broadcast, they seem to be the one most willing to take chances and try something new. They didn't say to us, 'This is an HD series and every frame must be created in HD.' Not surprisingly, what we found is that the content is king, and as long as the overall piece is framed in 16:9 people don't really mind that there are some images that are softer or funkier than the HD frames.

"In fact, the mixing of different production media provides a far more interesting effect than using straight High Definition video alone. Certain images should look funky with this sort of material. It's still a lot easier to achieve certain effects in NTSC or film than it is in High Definition. If you can do the postproduction for these effects before you bump it up to HD you can save yourself a whole lot of money and have a whole lot of fun."

Final Impressions

"Ideally, the technology used to produce programming should be transparent to the producers as well as the viewers. Ordinarily, a series like this would be shot using Super16 or Betacam. In this case High Definition video was mandated by our production partner. I think what's really captured people about *NYOTE* is that we haven't let the difficulties in working in High Definition video hamper us very much.

"Before we started working on *NYOTE* there had never really been any programming in High Definition video that dealt with harsh reality in High Definition video like *NYOTE* does. If you look at the history of High Definition video programming it's primarily been stuff that's been arts oriented, topics that takes advantage of High Definition video's ability to produce beautiful and colorful images. With *NYOTE,* the idea was to show an urban landscape in all its grittiness—a reality-based program that would use this incredibly accurate imaging medium to portray the darker side of life in the city that never sleeps.

"There were actually very few times that I felt that there were shots we couldn't get in High Definition. When we did run into these situations, such as in the subway tunnels or in some nightclub locations that were too cramped, too crowded, too dark, or where the spontaneity we needed would have been compromised, we opted to shoot in Betacam or Hi-8 and upconvert it. For *Hackers,* the episode on taxicab drivers, we needed to record conversations between the cabbies and the passengers as well as get POV shots from the driver's seat. The only way to get these shots was with a lipstick camera, and there was no point in recording it in High Definition, even if we could. It didn't matter in the end that it wasn't shot in High Definition video because viewers have come to expect these kinds of shots to look grainier and funkier."

For more information, see *New York: On The Edge* beginning on page 98.

Mark Forker

Mark started out professional life as a photographer, and went on to do postproduction for artists who had received grants from the NEA and the New York State Council on the Arts. From there he moved to Philadelphia and got interested in effects editing, building a reputation for innovative work that landed him a job at Charlex in Manhattan. Mark left Charlex to join REBO in 1989, and after several years moved to Los Angeles to become the chief editor at HDLA. In 1994, Mark joined Digital Domain doing effects work on Apollo 13 *and* Waterworld, *among other projects. He is currently an effects supervisor there.*

"In the early days of HDTV, preproduction and production meant everything to the success of a project. When I started as an effects editor at REBO, we were still very limited by the lack of postproduction tools—especially when compared to what I took for granted in NTSC. So, the most important task before going into production was previsualization, to see a special effects scene all the way from shooting it to the edit, taking into account the tools we had in the edit room.

"Barry Rebo's vision was to make producing High Definition video a postproduction process as much as a production process. The whole idea of my coming to REBO was to bring techniques from more traditional video special effects postproduction into High Definition video and integrate them as well as we could.

"My first High Definition video project was *Leaves Home*, directed by Cosimo, a commercial for Sony (see *Leaves Home* beginning on page 80). In that spot, even though extensive previsualization of the effect (which was to lift a house off its foundation) was done, one of the things that wasn't taken into account was what was going to happen to the light when the shoot ended up taking longer than scheduled. At the end of the day, the camera was pointing literally at the sun, but we needed to continue shooting because we hadn't got all the shots we needed. To get rid of the sun, we had to flag off the camera, but the flags were visible in the shot and we needed to replace this sky with sky taken from earlier in the day.

"On another day, when we were shooting close ups, we were hoping that the sky would be the right blue for keying with the Ultimatte so we could use the early sky from the previous day's shoot. But it was a completely gray overcast day. What we needed to do was combine elements from these two shoot days, and the lack of blue sky meant a change in thinking.

"Without any postproduction graphics tools, these production problems normally would have meant extending the shoot another day to get things right. Fortunately, however, the REBO ReStore was far enough along to use. (Editor's note: The ReStore™ is a dual-buffer High Definition video-resolution graphics device with real time digitizing capability, digital mixers, and alpha channel matting capability. It uses a Macintosh computer as the host, and is designed to be compatible with virtually all Macintosh graphics software.) The ReStore gave us a lot of postproduction options we never had before. With it we grabbed still frames, and using ColorStudio—this was before Photoshop came out—used a variety of techniques including rotoscoping and cut-and-paste to fix and combine bad and missing elements. We then recorded the stills back out to tape, and we were able to composite the elements together. While this is common in NTSC postproduction, it was a breakthrough for HDTV.

"Even when you have previsualized an effect and you know you're going to have all the right equipment and the right people on the shoot, things still go wrong. A little bit of research and testing can go a long way towards clarifying your thinking. Previsualizing an effect doesn't mean just thinking it through in your head. A simple test, even using something as low tech as Hi-8, can go a long way to letting you know if you can achieve the effect you want, the way you've planned it. The simplest way to do things is to do them simply at first, proving to yourself that it really does work the way you think it does.

"Right after *Leaves Home* for Sony, we did a commercial for Kentucky Fried Chicken. We were sitting in a meeting with the client and the director they had hired and they were telling us how to create the primary effect—which was to make an actor look like a ghost—because they'd made ghosts hundreds of times in NTSC and film. I said, 'Well, you haven't done ghosts in High Definition before and I haven't either. I want to do some tests first to find out if there is a better way to do it.'

"We set up a camera in somebody's office and shot some tests. To the client's, the agency's, and the director's surprise, we ended up approaching the job differently from the way they thought it had to be done. It ended up taking exactly the same amount of time it would have taken had we done it the way they insisted it had to be done, but we shot the whole commercial against black instead of blue or green. This gave us the ability to create an unusual solid quality to the ghostly image in post, using multiple passes and different layering techniques.

"But increasingly in High Definition, as in other media, just about anything can be fixed or created in post now that tools like Flame (from Discreet Logic) are available. These are frame-by-frame tools that do not work in real time, so they lack much of the immediacy of conventional video postproduction techniques, but more and more work is being done this way. Besides, it's only a matter of time before they will work in real time.

"It's a good example of understanding what peoples' expectations for High Definition video must be, because they can see the picture on the screen and they look at the tools and they say, 'These are video tools and I work in video. It's just that the image is bigger.' But then they often come to the realization that High Definition is a new art form, and that the manufacturers haven't come out with all of the colors they want and the brushes they are used to using, and they have to figure out how to make art anyway.

"People should be really excited about High Definition because it really does offer them a third format alternative. The transition from big screen to the television screen brought about the development a whole new visual language, and a whole new set of tools came into being. Like most languages and tools, things kept evolving. Maybe the most evolved form of television visuals can be found on MTV. You can tell that the MTV look is successful because of the number of films that borrow from it. Directors and artists moved into television because a new language—a new art form—had been created, and now it's been absorbed into the older art form, film.

"In the last couple of years, games and interactive multimedia have created another new place for artists to drive the creation of a new language and art form. Again there's another set of tools and possibilities, and another type of person who says, 'This is exciting to me. How I can make images?'

"This opportunity exists in High Definition video, too. Although it looks a lot like television, it combines all the positive aspects of film and all the positive aspects of television into one medium. Whereas some people say, 'You'll never replace film,' or, 'You'll never replace video,' the fact of the matter is that High Definition video is not a replacement for either of those media; it's a whole new medium to work in with its own advantages that create its own opportunities.

"I'm working on a 3D ride film project right now that's a good example. If we could take grain and jitter out of the film, we would because they are hindering the process of making a better final production. The stereo images have to be projected across a huge theater in 65mm film, and if the images are off by the equivalent of more than 4 pixels the stereo imaging isn't going to be as good as it really needs to be. The only way to guarantee the kind of alignment we need would have been to work in High Definition video.

"High Definition video is this new medium that produces the finest picture available on a monitor. Here I am (at Digital Domain) constantly working on these big beautiful film images, but I hadn't seen a High Definition monitor in quite a while. When I went back to HDLA, I was like every single client that came into the edit room for the first time in the five years that I worked at REBO. I was blown away; it was like looking through a window to me again and I hadn't seen that for a while. Film looks cool, but High Definition video images look unlike anything else. They both have their place; they're both king of their own domain."

Philip Hack

Philip has been working in High Definition video for about six years, directing, producing, or engineering on all types of programs, from the 1994 NFL Super Bowl *to* World Cup Soccer, *NBA* All-Star Basketball, Woodstock '94, The Gypsy Kings Live at Wolftrap, *and* Victor/Victoria *on Broadway—with stops at Sumo tournaments along the way.*

On Producing and Directing Live Sporting Events

"What *are* the challenges and realities faced when shooting sports in High Definition video? First of all, the most obvious thing that you notice in sports is that the 16:9 aspect ratio of High Definition video fits most sports playing surfaces quite nicely. Football, basketball, soccer, and even hockey fit naturally into the shape of the High Definition frame. This means that you can see more of the field when you're not shooting as wide. The wider aspect ratio also means that you can watch *all* of a play develop along the length of the field.

"In NTSC you often can't see all of the players from the game camera. In High Definition video you can see everything. This means you don't need to cut as quickly. For example, when shooting basketball I can have one shot that covers from the shot clock to the top of the key. From that one shot, it's possible to watch a team work together as a unit rather than focusing on one or two central players. The game camera can frame more loosely on the player with the ball. From the standpoint of the fan watching the game on TV it's great. They get to see everything that's going on. They can watch the whole team, or both teams, not just have their attention focused on just one or a few players.

"As a director I find I don't need as many different camera angles because there's so much more going on in each shot. You get to see many more subtleties than you can in NTSC. One detail that I really like, especially in basketball and football, is the ability to see a player's eyes when they give a head fake just before giving another player the shake and bake. Fans get a better idea what it means to be a defender because of this.

On the 1995 NBA *All-Star Game*

"I produced and directed the 1995 NBA *All-Star Game* and NBA *Stay in School Jam* (a co-production between Cinema of the Future and NHK), which went live to several theatres around the country. For this production we used a total of six High Definition cameras; two Sony HDC–500 CCD cameras, three Sony HDC–300 tube cameras, and the new JVC KH-100U CCD camera. Three Sony HDD-1000 digital VTRs and one (analog) UNIHI VTR were used as record decks. Graphics, score updates, and player stats were provided by a High Definition Chyron Scribe and a REBO Research ReStore. The only effects we had available to use were switcher effects, wipes, and so forth.

"The two Sony 500 cameras were used as handhelds under the basket; one had a Fujinon 6x lens and the other a Nikon 7x lens. The tight camera (at mid court) was equipped with a Canon 40x lens, the game camera (also at mid court) had a Nikon 7x lens, the endzone camera used a 10x Nikon lens with a 2x extender, and the JVC camera, with its Nikon lens, was used primarily as the clock camera.

"We also used the JVC camera and a JVC W-VHS machine for remote production of the NBA *Fan Jam* the day before. That night the footage was edited into packages that were used for a full halftime show during the game. We also were able to use High Definition stock footage—including helicopter shots—for the show open.

"One aspect of the 1995 NBA *All-Star Game* that may have been the most significant breakthrough was that there was a live High Definition video transmission, via Pacific Bell fiber-optic telephone lines, to several United Artists theaters in California. It may not sound like much, but I think it's one of the first live sporting events in the United States to use High Definition ENG crews and prepackaged segments to provide the viewers with what they're used to seeing on a comparable NTSC show."

On the 1994 World Cup

"For the 1994 World Cup we shot six games over a period of two weeks, in Chicago at Soldier Field and in New Jersey at Giants Stadium. Two small trucks were used, one for production and video, and one for videotape and audio. Most of what we did was recorded to tape and then couriered to a location in California where it was sent via the High Definition MUSE transmission system to Tokyo for immediate broadcast. For some games, a live downconverted NTSC version of the program to Tokyo was also provided. In essence, we were sometimes originating two shows from a single source for two different audiences—a High Definition audience and an NTSC audience. I think this is a good example of one of the strengths of High Definition video.

"This dual origination requirement necessitated some interesting configurations. Because we were shooting in New Jersey and the commentators were in Japan, we had to change the feedback loop to accommodate each situation. Our local announcers were getting feedback from Tokyo during the High Definition tape-delayed games through the commentary control room of the European Broadcasting Union (the host broadcaster for The World Cup). During the games that were transmitted live, we needed to get feedback from our local announcers as well as from Tokyo, and it all needed to be routed through our truck. It doesn't really sound difficult until you try to change all of this very quickly and have only one chance to get it right.

"The World Cup was shot using two Sony HDC–300 cameras and one Sony HDC–500 camera, and recorded on two Sony HDD–1000 digital VTRs. The 500 camera was fitted with a Canon 40x lens. One of the 300 cameras had a Fujinon 22x lens and the other 300 was equipped with a Nikon 10x lens. Slow motion replays were provided by a specially modified Panasonic UNIHI VTR with dynamic tracking that was fed by an ISO from the switcher.

"Due to the cable lengths from the trucks to the camera, we used fiber-optic cables to connect the cameras. Each camera was typically 500 meters from the truck. That's about 1.5 miles of cable per location, not including backup. There is no way to use triax, which is a shame, because most sporting venues already have triax run to the camera positions. You can't just plug the truck into a patch panel and set up the cameras.

"With High Definition, you have the option of using multicore cable with a maximum length of about 250 meters, which is not long enough for sports events, or fiber-optic cables. This often means an extra day of work at each location laying cables. I've even had to break holes in concrete walls because arena designers never anticipated the need to run nonstandard cable.

"For The World Cup, the fiber-optic cables were shipped to the locations in advance and run by the EBU. Unfortunately, there were problems at both locations because the EBU crews were not used to laying the more fragile fiber-optics and the cables got damaged.

"The hardest part of producing The World Cup games was the schedule. Usually when you shoot in multiple locations you can leapfrog your equipment and staff. Because of the lack of equipment in the United States at the time, we needed to set up, shoot, travel two trucks twenty hours and start the process all over again, which may not sound so bad until you realize that you need to shoot again the next day! The equipment problem has been partly addressed by the complement of gear that HD VISION has down in Irving, Texas. This remedies the equipment issue, but that isn't necessarily the case in the dollar sense. A second High Definition video truck is still much more expensive than a second NTSC truck."

On Lens Availability

"Shooting sports for television requires long focal length lenses. Unfortunately, there aren't a lot of these lenses currently available for the Sony HDC–500 camera. Until recently, in fact, there were only two long lenses in the U.S. A Canon 40x15 lens, and a Fujinon 22x18 lens. The Canon gets you out to about 600mm and the Fujinon to about 400mm. The 40x is comparable in length to what you're used to using for NTSC now.

"But if you think I'm going to tell you that there's been a sudden influx of lenses available as a result of the sports production we've done, think again. As this is being written there's only one long lens available—the Fujinon lens has completed its trip and is now back in Japan. Fujinon also makes a 40x lens, but it has never been available in the United States as a rental item. This may be due to increased production demand in Japan.

"The limited availability of lenses also gets in the way when you're doing handhelds. There are only two or three true handheld lenses in the U.S.—a Fujinon 6x lens. It's lightweight, easy to operate, and very sharp. Unfortunately, I think there are only about seven or eight of them in the world, and I seem to have a hard time getting hold of them. Shooting handhelds with heavier lenses requires a stronger camera operator and more tweaking to make a comfortable mount.

It's much harder to hold the camera steady and level because it's heavier. In spite of this, I've had great success with handhelds."

On Lighting

"Thinking about lenses makes me think about lighting: 'How many footcandles will there be on the playing field?'

"In order to shoot at the tight ends of long lenses while maintaining focus, and still be able to use the extenders, there needs to be a lot of light. Available light presents a real challenge because focus is critical in sports. Following a football, soccer ball, or basketball flying through the air and keeping it in focus is next to impossible without the proper amount of light. For dramatic work, the demands are not quite as high, but in a sports environment you're not trying to hide anything or create a mood—you're trying to show everything. On shows where I feel we've gotten our best results, we've usually had about 175 to 250 footcandles on the playing surface. Fortunately, most of the newer stadiums and arenas have decent lighting.

"For a camera operator, following focus under less than ideal lighting conditions can be very difficult. This creates a dilemma. We want to use long lenses but we can't shoot tight with them because at the end of the lens, light falls off making it difficult to focus because there's no depth of field.

"This is in fact a problem, but it can be compensated for by shooting a little wider. These pictures, even though they are not as tight, are still quite awesome when they are projected on a large screen. In fact, a tight picture is sometimes a little too stimulating when it is projected large, and it becomes difficult to adjust to the game camera, which is usually a wider shot."

On Directing

"Cutting between extreme close-ups and wide shots is much more jarring in High Definition video than it is in NTSC. For this reason alone, it is necessary to think about coverage differently than in NTSC.

"I recently produced *The Gypsy Kings Live at Wolftrap*, a concert event that lasted several nights. On the first night, the director was cutting like the program was for MTV. In my opinion, it was a little too fast. That's not necessary when shooting High Definition video. For this performance there were thirteen musicians on stage, and it was possible to see every one of them in the wide shot. And you could see what every one of them was doing and how they were reacting to each other.

"In NTSC, you can't hang on a shot very long because there's just not much happening, or if you're wide, the detail is too small. With High Definition, you get to be more deliberate in the way you cut, and you can involve the viewer more by settling on a shot. You don't have to keep cutting to show the viewer what you think they should see. High Definition images contain so much detail that the viewers can scan the picture and participate more. They can watch what's going on in the frame without the director having to show it to them.

"There is another change in directing and camera work that occurs when shooting High Definition. The camera operators have to work harder. In NTSC coverage of a sporting event it's not unusual for there to be ten to fifteen cameras, and any one camera might be responsible for three or four shots during a game. A High Definition camera operator covering the same event might be responsible for six or seven or more shots. That doesn't leave much time for the camera operators to relax and rest their eyes.

"It's the little things like this—as well as the bigger picture, no pun intended—that make it more challenging to shoot in High Definition video. Directing sports in High Definition is made more difficult by the fact that the source monitors are usually very small, often only 10", and the program monitor is small as well, maybe18". In my own experience I find I have an easier time directing for a large screen when I'm looking at a large screen. I have a tendency to frame too tightly on the tight shots when I'm looking at small monitors. This is a common problem in sports, and one that will be worked out as more and more people become accustomed to directing in High Definition video."

Final Impressions

"One aspect of High Definition video that I especially like is that it really drags you into the game. You become much more involved because you really can see more. I say this from a production standpoint as well as from the viewers' standpoint. To me, watching video engineers who usually don't care at all about the content of a sporting event jumping up and down screaming at the monitor is a sign of the power of High Definition video.

"High Definition video can make even the most jaded people excited again. It's very rewarding to work with a crew that is truly excited about what they are doing and striving to do their best. My productions with numerous crews across the country has shown me that High Definition video really brings out the best in the game and in the people covering it. I know it sounds corny, but when the pictures look so good, people want to make them even better."

Keith Melton

Keith, co-owner for the past twelve years of Infinity Filmworks, has a broad background in film and video production—standard and large formats as well as High Definition video—that includes directing, writing, producing, working with advanced technology, and coordinating complex special effects.

"High Definition video technology comes closer than any other imaging technology to capturing and reproducing the way the human visual system sees the world. The 16:9 format fits in better with our horizontal view of the world, and the shape of HD is more interesting compositionally than the 4:3 of NTSC or PAL. Then there's the stereotypical 'window' effect, the impression that looking at an HD monitor is like looking through a window. This is a very visceral effect, and it prompts this exciting reaction from people when they look at HD. From a director or producer's point of view this excitement is fantastic because you just don't get it from film or conventional video.

"The problem, as far as producing or directing High Definition video, is that still today there's not enough support of the technology to push it to do things that conventional film or video technology can do for you. In some cases it seems like it's taking one step forward and two steps back. One step forward in the sense that the image is fantastic and unparalleled and unique in the way that we view the world, but two steps back because of the lack of postproduction tools we take for granted in conventional film and video.

"You have to be quite careful in what you create and how you create it in order to take advantage of HD and what it does best. For me, one really exciting use of HD is in computer graphics; creating all your effects in the digital realm and then transferring them to HD tape. This way you get the advantage of the look and the visual experience of HD, but you can create much more sophisticated looking images digitally than you can in film or NTSC video.

"That's what I did for a show for Panasonic called *Adventures in Audiana,* where the viewers travel into a land of music, and they journey through these different areas; a classical world, a jazz world, a blues world, and a rock and roll world, and it's created entirely of computer graphics environments and characters.

"The client was very happy. The technique was extremely effective, and the end result looked great. The visual style is unique; everyone looks at it and goes, 'Wow! What is that?'

"The result wasn't cartoony, even though it consisted entirely of computer graphics and used conventional cartoon animation techniques. By not transferring the final piece to film or video we didn't lose any of the look the original computer graphics had. When you transfer computer graphics to video or film it affects the digital look of the image because NTSC, PAL, and film reproduce color differently from HD. For this reason, HD is extremely interesting to the world of computer graphics because of its color saturation and its apparent depth.

"The most challenging project I was involved in, technically and artistically, was *To Dream of Roses* for Sumitomo Corporation for the 1990 Osaka Expo. Unfortunately, we—Doug Trumbull was the executive Producer—had to use analog VTRs on the shoot; the new digital VTRs were just breaking into the market, and they weren't available to us.

"What was interesting technically about *To Dream of Roses* was that we had two HD cameras rigged to two interlocked, manually controlled motion control systems. One camera shot dancers against a huge bluescreen, the other camera shot a scale miniature set. It ended up looking like the dancers were dancing in these really incredible environments. As the director, I could see everything live. I could see all the camera moves; I could plot things out. Plus, I had the ability to be more interactive and try things I might not have if I was shooting film.

"At one point we actually used some full-scale set pieces that perfectly matched the miniatures so the dancers could move in and amongst—actually within—the set. Then we added fog and other elements, even leaves on some trees that the dancers could play with so it seemed like they were physically interacting with the miniature set. And that worked very well. *To Dream of Roses* was transferred to 70mm. At the time we did this, there was no direct HD to 70mm transfer system, so the HD original was transferred to 35mm and then bumped up to 70mm.

"The next HD project I was involved in was the preshow for the *Sub Oceanic Shuttle* ride film for Iwerks Entertainment.

"HD was chosen for the preshow because Iwerks wanted the preshow to have a high-tech look; they wanted something that was unconventional, a preshow that didn't look like a traditional preshow. The *Sub Oceanic Shuttle* ride film itself was supposed to be some advanced technology, and they wanted to use an advanced image playback technology to get riders set up for the experience. The ride film itself was unusual in that it was 100% computer graphics directly imaged to 65mm negative film. This meant that a first generation 65mm print was running through the projector, a tremendous visual experience even without the HD preshow.

"Until the 1996 Tokyo Expo was cancelled, I was working with Iwerks Entertainment on the world's first interactive ride film. The film was to be a combination of computer graphics and live action, and it would have been shot on film and projected in High Definition. The point of a branching narrative film is to enable viewers to choose which of the possible storylines they want to experience. The key to that is random access, something you can't do with film but that you can do with videodiscs, and in this case High Definition videodiscs.

"These uses of High Definition video technology—projection systems, ride films—especially in small-sized venues seems to me to be a big and growing market. Not only is High Definition video more portable than film, you get a cleaner image at small sizes, especially when viewers are seated close to the screen.

"Going forward, I'm not very interested in using HD for shooting conventional live-action situations. For me, using HD is about doing something else besides just capturing the world. Let's affect the world and play with it in the HD format, that's what interests me.

"There's a truism when any new medium comes out, the first thing you try to do with it is to mimic old media. You need some time before you can sit down and actually say what is it that the medium can do which is unique to the medium or true to the inherent nature of the medium. We're still spending time, because of the relative lack of tools, doing things we know how to do already, rather than attempting to do things that we've not been able to do before."

Noriko T. Mukai

Noriko is HDTV & Interactive Media Producer for Tokyo Broadcasting System (TBS), producing programming for TBS High among other venues. She majored in both linguistics and communications at Ohio University and Tsukuba University in Japan. She has won three Astrolabium Awards for her work in High Definition video production from the International Electronic Cinema Festival.

"High Definition video is characterized not only by twice the number of scanning lines of standard television, but often twice or more the production costs of traditional video—depending on the content of the production. As a result, in the High Definition video production world we find a small number of very high budget productions with quality results, many low budget productions with mediocre results, and a great many production ideas abandoned at the planning stage due to a lack of adequate financing.

"Recently I acted as producer for *On the Far Side of Twilight*, a forty-minute drama with a production budget of approximately $650,000.

"The financing of the production began by first participating in, and winning, a software competition sponsored by Chiba City, which was interested in a promotional program for display at its High Definition video theaters and viewing locations. Further financing was found from an advertising firm interested in funding research and development in High Definition video software development, and from an electronics manufacturing firm in return for use of an edited version of the program as demonstration software for their High Definition video products.

"In the end, versions of *On the Far Side of Twilight* were created in Japanese, English, and French in High Definition video and on 35mm and 16mm film. Furthermore, two fifteen-minute versions were edited, both of them in Japanese and in High Definition video only, for demonstration purposes for the sponsors of the production. All of the costs for producing all of these versions, including original music and score, had to be accounted for in the $650,000 budget.

"Needless to say, we had to be very careful about how the money was used, and the methods used to make production dollars go a long way were, I believe, the result of a very open minded, flexible, and creative approach to technical applications.

"When faced with the sorts of challenges we faced in producing *On the Far Side of Twilight*, it is important for the producer, the director, and the cinematographer to get together and discuss very carefully, before actually starting the production, the methods that would be used to produce each shot in the production. For each scene in *On the Far Side of Twilight* we asked the following questions:

> What was the artistic intent or the desired effect we were searching for? For example, did it require a soft, dreamy image or a harder-edged feeling of reality?
>
> What ways were available for us to achieve the desired effect?
>
> What was the most cost-effective way to achieve the desired effect without sacrificing the creative intent?

"Based on the outcome of these discussions it was decided that origination should take place in a combination of media; High Definition video, 35mm film, 16mm film, Betacam SP, and PaintBox. Multiple source origination of footage was the result of weighing the artistic intent of each scene against the cost-efficiency in both production and postproduction stages. Multiple source origination enabled us to cut production costs considerably.

"*On the Far Side of Twilight* was shot in nine days. Seven days were spent shooting outdoors and on location, and the remaining two days were spent in the studio, primarily shooting bluescreen.

"35mm film was chosen for much of the background scenery in the imaginary sequences for its very soft, dreamy effect. About 15% of the production was originated on 35mm film. 16mm film was chosen for its grainy texture, and was used for dream sequences. About 7% of the production was originated on 16mm film. Betacam SP was used for one sequence that used fixed-point observational shooting (time lapse) of a tree as it was undergoing changes through the seasons. PaintBox was used to enhance a cloudy and rainy sky for the end sequence. High Definition was the origination medium for the remainder of the production.

"Most of the techniques used in postproduction were very simple, classic, and straightforward. Rather than overwhelming the viewer with flashy 3D computer graphics we used simple digital video effects that were more in tune with the feeling of the piece and were far less expensive than 3D effects.

"We often hear that High Definition has more than five times the visual information of standard NTSC. At the same time, the defects and sacrifices made are five times as apparent in High Definition. Therefore, it is important to be very careful when weighing production choices. The key to success in achieving cost-effective production methods is to have a very close working relationship between the producer, director, and cinematographer."

Jay Schmalholz

Jay is a freelance producer/director who has focused on sports—especially alternative "adrenaline" sports—for the past three years. He was on the staff of MTV Sports for two years.

On Producing Adrenaline Sports in High Definition Video

"REBO approached the company I work for (Vogue Fish Productions) to see if the MTV style of shooting adrenaline sports would translate to High Definition video for a program called *Hyperactive: Radical Sports* for one of their clients, TBS (Tokyo Broadcasting System).

"The MTV style of sports coverage is very different from normal sporting coverage. Like much of the rest of the programming on the channel, it's very intense with lots of rapid edits in both the video and the audio. REBO wanted to get an hour of this kind of intensity covering four different sports, and within each sport, four different elements of that sport. We were successful to a degree, but limitations imposed by the budget, schedule, and equipment made it impossible to exactly duplicate what we would do using standard equipment."

On Preproduction

"Although we had been in discussions with REBO and TBS for about two months on the project, getting to know the requirements of the project and learning some of the limitations of the equipment, there was only about a week from the time we got the green light to the time shooting started. A week is not a lot of time to outline the stories, scout and get permits for all of the necessary locations (over 40 of them), and secure all of the on-camera talent.

"One of the things that the short preproduction schedule meant was there wasn't enough time to test the camera or to visit the locations with camera to test for RF and other problems. RF turned out to be a real problem on this production because the—brand new!—camera we were using was, for some reason, more sensitive to RF than other models of the same camera that REBO had used before."

On Production

"One thing we tried to do with the High Definition video was to take advantage of the widescreen format. If you're using a format that's so beautiful, you want to at least sit on shots once in a while. MTV Sports almost never uses a shot that is more than five seconds long. In this project, to take advantage of widescreen, we broke out of that mold, and tried a combination of rhythms, bring the pace up and then bringing it down by using longer shots—in some places twenty seconds long. We consciously tried to break away from the MTV Sports format and strike a balance between that and a more traditional documentary style. I think there is room for that kind of experimentation in High Definition video.

"The question for me is, 'How 'authentic' does a High Definition video program have to be? Does it all have to be shot in High Definition video?'

"Preserving the look of video is not important in an MTV Sports-style program. I don't think everything needs to look the same, it gets a bit flat. I think you need to pop different elements. So we try to shoot film as much as possible, but we design in a lot of Hi-8. Sometimes we don't even shoot any Betacam at all, because after Hi-8 is tweaked a little bit it's difficult to tell the difference. Plus Hi-8 is a lot cheaper.

"For this production we ended up using standard 8mm video and 8mm film to shoot those elements we just couldn't get in High Definition video and designed a graphic treatment to insert the 4:3 elements into the 16:9 frame. We bounced the 8mm video off the film and High Definition video, playing the different looks of the media off each other. The question is, 'Will High Definition aficionados out there discount the program because of the inclusion of 8mm video and film that's been bumped up?'

"Right now, shooting with High Definition video equipment is not as quick or as efficient as the tools we normally use to produce this type of programming. One huge difference is that the camera operator is not in control, the engineer is, and it's tough getting the communication between the camera operator and the engineer to work for you.

"In an adrenaline sports program, almost everything you shoot happens very quickly and it's not set up, it happens on the fly. You've got a skater in a ramp or athletes jumping out of planes or kayaking down a waterfall. Thing just happens, and you're just not going to get those shots on HD right now: If a kayak tips over, the camera operator has got to have control to roll when they want to roll.

"That's one of the things that was frustrating about shooting in Sheep's Meadow in Central Park—which isn't extreme at all. But there are a lot of different things going on. Maybe there's a guy playing guitar, but to catch that, you have to tell the engineer you want to roll tape and then stand by. It's a beautiful shot, but in the fifteen seconds or so it takes to talk to the engineer and get the tape up to speed, the subject might move. It got to the point where I said, 'I don't care how much tape we're burning, just let it roll.' I didn't want people to realize that the camera was there. I wanted to be able to catch people off guard and be able to capture that moment.

"Being connected by a camera cable is a restriction I had never encountered before. The camera operator used to shooting with a small film camera or a camcorder doesn't feel as mobile. It's a mental thing, the camera operators know they're connected to the VTR by a cable and can't move as freely.

"If we had more time in preproduction, we would have figured out more ways to rig the camera and VTR to get them more mobile. The cart that the REBO engineers set up was more manageable than I thought it would be, but still, we couldn't keep up with inline skaters zipping through a line of cones. That would be trouble with any camera rig when you're trying to get really creative to get inside the sport and feel the action."

On Postproduction

"Postproduction was not very different than it would be for an extreme sports-style show shot using film and standard video only. We used a nonlinear video editing system in both cases, and all of the source material gets digitized anyway. The downconversion and digitizing process did make it difficult to see the shots with RF in them. If we had more time, we would probably have designed some sort of effect that used the RF to give the video a textured or distressed look that would turn the 'problem' into something that looked intentional. But that approach may not work for other types of programs."

Final Impressions

"I loved working with the large format. That was probably the most intriguing thing about the whole shoot for me.

"I'd never shot widescreen before; I've always shot 4:3, even in film. What was fun was filling the frame, thinking in thirds instead of halves; left and right and center, and trying to fill that whether it was an interview or a beauty shot or an action shot. It was more difficult; things have to be a lot more choreographed to fill that frame. But we all saw the beauty of the shape of the frame.

"I don't know a lot about the technical side of HD or about the politics of it, but from a creative viewpoint, I can see the potential. We came to a new medium, a new format, and it forced us to do things we would not have done otherwise.

"The word about High Definition video is not really out yet. My only experience with it is has been this one project. In fact, I'd never even seen any High Definition video before I worked on this project. There's a whole world out there to shoot in HD. I think we only scratched the surface. There's a lot more we could have done with more time and more money—but that's the case on almost every production."

Neil Smith

Neil was one of the founding partners of REBO Production Associates and was with REBO until 1993, when he left to pursue a career as an independent director. During his tenure at REBO, Neil was a lighting director, DP, director, and creative director, participating in dozens of High Definition video productions.

On Lighting for Bluescreen

"The primary goal in lighting a bluescreen background is to make sure that the blue is evenly lighted. In order to pull the best matte in post, you want the blue to be as even as possible. The less even the lighting job, the more work you have to do in the edit room tweaking the Ultimatte to generate the key. The more work you have to do generating the key, the more the foreground image deteriorates.

"The first two generations of High Definition video cameras (the Sony HDC–100 and HDC–300) were quite slow—we rated them about 64 to 80 ASA. This is about 2 stops slower than the current camera, the HDC–500. Using the 100 or 300 camera meant using a lot of light—four times more light than is needed when using a 500 camera—which made it quite difficult to get the blue evenly lighted. But that was then and this is now. With the 500, lighting blue requires no more work than for a film or for standard video.

"When we were shooting *Fool's Fire* (see *Fool's Fire* beginning on page 89), the problem was the reverse; we were working in very low light conditions most of the time, shooting both film (Eastman 5296, which is rated at a conservative 500 ASA) and High Definition video. I remember one scene where the foreground was lighted at about 25 to 35 footcandles (FC), which is pretty low. You can imagine that at that low light level for the foreground that it was very difficult to get the blue, which was very close to the actors, evenly lighted. It is so easy to get spill from a light that can cause a four or five FC hotspot. Five FC wouldn't really matter if the wall were being lighted at 150 FC, but it was a really big problem at 25."

On Achieving the Right Look

"I consider High Definition video to be an electronic form of 35mm film and all of the techniques that can used in 35mm film production to achieve the look that a production demands can—and should—be used when shooting in High Definition.

"On the shoots I've been on, the cameras have been on trains, planes, automobiles, boats, canoes, helicopters, and motorcycles. They've been used on Panaflexes, Panatates, jib arms, dollies, and Steadicams—and even underwater. We've done just about everything with a High Definition camera that you can do with a 35mm camera.

"But the designers of the original cameras were thinking video not film, and using filters with video is something that very few video DPs or camera operators have any experience with or think about. Those who do, usually come from the film world. But using filters is one of the new creative opportunities that High Definition video offers.

Figure 7.1—Rigging the Sony HDC–500 with a matte box

You can use filters very effectively to create mood and special effects, and if you're not using them when you shoot High Definition video, you're wasting a vast creative opportunity. Right after we (REBO) got our first cameras, we had them modified and had Arriflex build special adapters so we could use a 6.6 matte box.

"When you are using filters, it is important to discuss what you're doing with the engineer. For example, if you've decided on a certain look that requires a light diffusion filter, let the engineer know. If the engineer is not a part of the discussion, or is not paying attention, or does not have a capable eye, then it's a simple matter to reduce or completely negate the effects of the diffusion filter by playing with the detail enhancement control on the CCU. So, when you diffuse High Definition video, it's a combination of the electronic controls in the CCU and the optical effects of the filter itself."

Final Impressions

"In my experience, the Sony HDC–500 camera should really be rated at 320 ASA. When you push the gain on the 500, it is possible go all the way out to 2000 ASA but the blacks wash out and fill up with video noise, and you lose a lot of detail. But that's not necessarily bad—it's a look. I remember lighting a scene with just a soft light bouncing off a wall and got this really beautiful picture. I pulled out my meter and it read fifteen FC. It worked, though.

"In some ways it's like shooting with film. Although a stock might be rated by the manufacturer at 500, you may find that exposing it at 650 gives you the look you want. So, for you, the stock is rated at 650.

"If you're looking for the highest quality NTSC program and you want it to look like video and not film, shoot it in High Definition and downconvert it to NTSC. You'll get all the quality you associate with 35mm film and all the convenience of video. It will look better than if you shot the production on BetaSP and edited it in D1. If you still need more of a 'film look,' there's always the option to transfer your High Definition footage to film."

Siegfried Steiner

Siegfried Steiner founded Steiner Film, located in Grünewald, Germany, near Munich ("Just like Hollywood and Beverly Hills," says Siegfried) in 1968. Long considered a pioneer in adapting new technologies to 35mm film production, Steiner Film specializes in television commercials and corporate production, and has extensive experience shooting in Showscan (60 fps 65mm), 70mm, and Cinemascope formats. They have also done feature-length production in High Definition video.

On His First Experience Shooting High Definition Video

"I first shot High Definition video in 1989. Sony came to us and loaned us the equipment to use in a production. I'd never even touched a video camera until 1988; since I started my company, I'd only used 35mm film equipment. Sony brought everything in an OB (outside broadcast) van all the way from England for this shoot. When I first saw the equipment, I remember seeing the camera and this big zoom lens—I never used zoom lenses—and thinking, 'We're not shooting a soccer game here, we're shooting a car commercial.' I asked them to pack it up without even waiting to try it out.

"Well, they didn't go away, and as we started setting up for the shoot like we always do, the Sony people started setting up the HDC–300 near the 35mm camera. As we were lighting the set, my camera assistant went and looked in the OB van, came over to me, and suggested that I go take a look—because it wasn't looking that bad. I went and looked myself and it was pretty close to what I wanted it to look like. So I said it was okay for them to shoot after we got done setting up the lighting and shooting in 35mm.

"Lighting is very important for car commercials. When you light a car in the studio, if you change your viewpoint by as little as an inch, the light on the car changes because of all of the reflective surfaces. When you look at the car through the 35mm film camera's viewfinder, it's so small you can't really judge it exactly. But the High Definition monitor is big enough, and you can see exactly what you're seeing through the lens of the camera. You have to remember, when you're shooting in film, that you can never see the picture as you shoot it, you can only feel it. You never know what you're going to get until the film comes back from the lab.

"The Sony engineers rigged a monitor on the set, and, as the day went on, we started lighting the car not from the point of view of the film camera, but I started using the High Definition monitor to place and focus the lights. This was the first time I saw that there might be something different and useful in High Definition—it was a way to light better.

"For all of the first day we shot everything both on 35mm and in High Definition. We continued to shoot that way the following morning, but by the afternoon we were using only the High Definition equipment. So, it only took me about one and one-half days to get into the fascination of High Definition.

"After the studio shoot, we had to shoot the car on a test track—using the OB van. Normally we use a specially modified Citroën that has a crane with a 360 degree head that can get from ground level up to a height of 5 meters. When we got around to shooting the tracking shots we had to run the camera cable from the camera car to the OB van, both of which were pacing the car we were shooting. We had a person in the camera car whose job it was to guide the camera cable and make sure it didn't get in the way or damaged.

"And, because we were shooting outdoors in the bright sunlight, we had problems with comet tailing. We ended up reshooting all of the outdoor stuff on film. What took three days to do in High Definition took less than one and one-half days in film.

"What we learned was that, while High Definition was absolutely okay in the studio, there were problems shooting outside that we needed to solve.

"We presented the film to the client for the first time in High Definition on a High Definition monitor, and they were all impressed. They were seeing their car in a way they'd never seen it before. It wasn't film and it wasn't video. We transferred the High Definition to 35mm film, and even though it was 1989 and the transfer process hadn't been perfected, it looked really nice. It looked like film but it wasn't film, and it wasn't video—it was different, it was something special.

"We made the decision to buy a complete High Definition video production package after this first shoot we did. It was not an easy decision because it was so expensive. For a while, we shot projects using both High Definition video and film, using film where it was necessary for technical or logistical reasons. However, since the UNIHI VTR became available, we shoot everything in High Definition. Underwater shots. We even have a special mount to shoot 3D from our helicopter."

On Producing 3D Films in High Definition

"After I saw my first 3D image in High Definition, I immediately decided to do a film in 3D. Before then, when I'd seen 3D in film I always got a headache. This is because the two film images are never stable enough. The gates in the cameras and projectors are different, and the film for each moves differently. That's not the case with High Definition, it's very stable. In places where there is a large format projection system already installed, we are experimenting with printing both High Definition frames side by side on the same piece of film for projection."

On Shooting His First Feature, *The Phantom King's Diamond*

"The biggest thing we have ever done in High Definition was for Austrian television (ORF), a 90 minute fairy tale, *The Phantom King's Diamond*. It was also the first feature film we had ever done.

"The project was already set to be shot on 35mm film when some producers from NHK brought representatives from ORF to our office to show them what High Definition was capable of. After the meeting and many, many phone calls, we ended up becoming the producers.

"The main thing about the story was that it was a fairy tale not a real story. To achieve the effect we wanted, we did all of the principal photography, which took seven weeks, on a bluescreen set with minimal props and created the environments using 3D computer graphics. To realistically combine the live action actors with the computer-generated backgrounds, we built a special motion control system that enabled us to be far more interactive than if we had people moving a dolly and jib arm. This system also provided us with 3D positional data for the camera movements for the 3D computer graphics system, which made it easy to synchronize the background to the actors' movements and to render the backgrounds in the proper perspective.

"It took one year to produce the finished film, and in this time we produced about 40 minutes of 3D computer animation at High Definition resolution, which is a lot. We used proprietary software based on software originally by Robert Abel, running on an Alliant supercomputer. We bought a new Alliant for this production—the last one the company built before they went out of business.

"The premiere of *The Phantom King's Diamond* was in held Vienna in a theater where this kind of,fairy tale is normally performed live. There were about 1,000 people in attendance, including the top level of the Austrian film and video community. The program was projected on a 12 meter wide screen using four High Definition video projectors and five-channel surround sound. The result was incredible. Someone came up to me afterwards and told me they thought it was the best 70mm film projection they'd ever seen."

On Clients' Acceptance of High Definition in Europe

"On the whole, our commercial and corporate clients are much better off using High Definition than 35mm film. We feel we can provide them with a better product for the same price.

"The picture quality of High Definition provides my company with a unique edge. When another company tries a similar shot on film, it just looks better in High Definition. When 35mm film is transferred to conventional video, it loses a lot of quality, especially sharpness and color. When we shoot commercials on High Definition they have a different look than if they were shot on film, and the High Definition commercial will get more interest from viewers.

"Some agencies don't want to use High Definition because they are comfortable with the look of film—especially the grain. What they don't realize is the effect that film grain has on postproduction now that using computer programs like Flame to do compositing is very common. Unless you work at very high resolutions when transferring film to digital format—which you normally can't do because commercial budgets usually aren't big enough—the film grain is larger than the pixels. When you try to do motion tracking using complex mattes for compositing this can be a real problem in film. You don't have these problems with High Definition video. You can always add the film grain back in during postproduction in High Definition. Any kind of film grain you want.

"One added bonus our clients receive using High Definition is that they can use the images for print; catalogs and advertising. When we give clients digital files in TIFF format, they can select from the 30 frames per second we shoot exactly the image they want. We could never do that from the 35mm films that we were shooting. There are a lot of special promotion catalogs that have been done entirely from High Definition images we shot, and the clients are saving money because they didn't have to pay for a separate shoot with a still photographer. The first time we sent a TIFF file off to a printer, they called us back and asked us what digital photography system we were using; the video still cameras that they'd seen were not nearly as good."

Final Impressions

"The equipment you use is only one part of a production; the important part is how you create the image with the equipment you have. To use High Definition video equipment well takes some experience, but with High Definition video you have more possibilities to create something different—and something nicer. When we are shooting in some difficult conditions or a special location I might ask my assistant, 'How would we do this on film?' Sometimes he'll say to me, 'We might not get it.' There are many examples in the work we do of scenes you'd never get on film."

Chapter 8

Life after NTSC

As this book goes to press, it seems obvious that there will be life after NTSC. It may be HDTV, it may be ATV, EDTV (Enhanced Definition Television) or it may be SDTV (Standard Definition Television), but there will be something more than—better than—what we know, and watch, and produce with right now.

Figure 8.1—Vietnamese children react to High Definition video production gear

"Whatever format is chosen," says Barry Rebo, "these new and expanded forms of television will definitely be in the marketplace within the next two years."

REBO's plan is to create a High Definition pay-per-view programming service in conjunction with TVN Entertainment, Inc., their partner in our Los Angeles-based postproduction facility, HDLA. At present, TVN offers a 24 hour a day multichannel pay-per-view movie service that is available to the over 4 million C-band satellite dish owners.

"It's no mystery that you don't garnish much prestige from a $10,000 car these days," says Rebo, "but the home with a $10,000 High Definition home entertainment center is the home that the neighbors will definitely want to come and visit.

"There certainly seem to be enough people with the purchasing power either to purchase outright or to lease such a system. We think that the 4 million C-band satellite dish owners represent such an interested television viewing audience, and they have already demonstrated their economic ability to purchase higher priced home theater systems.

"This presupposes, of course, that there will be something for these people to watch. At the moment, the largest volume of High Definition-compatible programming exists in the world's feature film libraries. Because of the way funding for High Definition video production is set up in Europe, the majority of non real time events produced in High Definition video are cultural programs that will translate well to the American market, and the majority of the programming is inherently evergreen. Furthermore, most of the production can be converted quite easily to a format suitable for broadcast over a C-band satellite. So we envision that the early High Definition programming services, including our own, will offer a mix of programming, with approximately 80 percent pay-per-view movie rentals and the balance being special events, sports, music, culture."

These home systems will consist of a big widescreen projection television with an HDTV decoder that can be connected to their existing satellite dish. In addition to being able to receive programming via satellite, owners of these systems will be able to add a W-VHS VCR and/or a digital video disk system.

In addition to satellite distribution into the home, another early market for High Definition Video is in what are commonly called 'Electronic Cinemas.' Typically, these electronic cinemas will be public venues, either part of a multiplex or a stand-alone theater, that will have the ability to downlink, via satellite or fiber-optic connection, live High Definition video signals as well as play back prerecorded programming.

Companies that are working to create electronic cinemas envision them as 200-seat venues with screen sizes of approximately 20 feet diagonal. Pacific Bell is experimenting with fiber distribution of High Definition Video programming right now. United Artists, as a part of its Prometheus project, is also experimenting by building a High Definition video 'compatible' system (typically a high scan rate projecter and an NTSC line-doubling system) into one theater of a multiplex. These venues are primarily for busines-to-business videoconferencing use during business. Irrespective of their use, or the method of distribution, aggressive electronic cinema business plans predict as many as 5000 screens around the country by the end of the decade.

There are similar High Definition video electronic cinemas installed in Europe—especially in France—where small- to medium-sized cities have installed HD receive-only equipment to receive programming originating from Paris and other major cultural centers. The 1994 World Cup was uplinked live from the United States to approximately 20 cities throughout France using this network.

"REBO is currently developing such an electronic cinema concept for museums and performing art centers throughout North America," says Barry Rebo, "with the goal of initiating five sites by mid 1996."

The programming mix, which will be distributed via satellite, will be targeted to a cultural demographic. Music, dance, theater, classic film programs, some live events, as well as "art-house" fare appear to be a natural fit for this demographic. "We think this is going to play better outside of the major markets," continues Rebo, "because a lot of the smaller markets can't attract a lot of major touring acts."

"The point is," says Rebo, "that the technology is no longer the inhibiting factor in the equation. All of the technology exists. It's still a matter of the economics of the apropriate price point per installation. We think we've got that part licked if we can develop a consistent stream of programs and events that will motivate people to leave their homes.

"It's interesting to note, with the privatization of television, originally in Europe but quickly spreading throughout Asia, that new television services and systems can become wildly profitable with between three to five million customers. Take Canal+ in France, for example. Ten years ago they set out to offer a premium service and set a cap of five million French customers. Even this relatively small number of customers (by American standards) provided significant profits to expand into other European communities. The lesson here is that the future is probably not in 'free' television, it's by offering the consumer quality and convenience, not sheer quantity.

"I think it's ironic that the FCC is being pressured by broadcasters to adopt multichannel standard definition television as opposed to offering quality in a more modest number of channels. People have enough crap TV; what they really want is quality. And people will pay for it."

The technology for fueling interest in, and the growth of, High Definition video production is also at a crossroads, although the path is becoming much clearer as to which direction development is going to take.

Figure 8.2—On location in Azerbaijan

Because Japan will host the 1998 Winter Olympics, Japanese broadcast equipment supply companies are highly motivated to reduce the size and cost of the next generation of High Definition video production equipment. Publicly stated goals include the development of High Definition video equipment that will cost only one-third more than their current top of the line NTSC and PAL counterparts. Perhaps even more exciting news is that prototype High Definition video camcorders are likely in this same time frame. This means that the disparity in cost between NTSC and HD production will diminish significantly. Furthermore, the availability of High Definition video camcorders will make it much easier to produce many styles of programming that are currently quite difficult.

> "What we're seeing," says Barry Rebo, "is that the development of the electronic cinema tools which people have envisioned as replacements or supplements to 35mm film production is actually being driven by Japanese broadcast demands that they become utilitarian TV production tools.
>
> "The next generation of High Definition video production equipment clearly reflects that dynamic. The emphasis on their use as a replacement or supplement for film is being clearly downplayed—at least in the short term. The reality is that the need to fill a daily twelve-hour High Definition video programming schedule demands greater flexibilty and less painful economics than the dream of digital electronic cinema production to replace 35mm film.
>
> "This equipment will be great for the home, and it will be more than suitable for projection in public venues; it may not be great for feature film producton. That really depends on the type of production, however. This new generation of equipment will almost certainly be a significant competitor to Super 16mm blown up to 35mm. It's also important to remember that *El Mariachi*, *The Brothers McMullen*, and *Hoop Dreams*—all critically acclaimed films—were shot in NTSC and blown up to 35mm film for theatrical release. It's going to be the new high def nickelodeon. It'll be a bunch of mavericks trying to figure it out."

Which just goes to show you that where there's a will and no budget there's still a way.

Postscript

On December 12th, 1995, during the final stages of completing the manuscript for this book, the FCC finally announced a decision on an Advanced Television transmission standard. The announcement, however, does not mean that the path to widespread adoption of Advanced Television will be smooth.

Among the issues still to be decided include the length of time that broadcasters will have to make the transition between standard definition television and Advanced Television. The original plan called for phasing out standard definition television broadcasts in the year 2112, but the transition period may be changed to end as early 2007 in order to reclaim the existing spectrum for reassignment.

Also under discussion is whether or not broadcasters will be required to use the additional spectrum space they will be allocated for Advanced Television to provide High Definition video programming, or even if broadcasters will be required to use their channels for television programming at all. At the heart of the matter is the fact that the digital compression technology that makes it possible to squeeze a High Definition video signal into 6MHz also makes it possible to squeeze six NTSC-resolution signals into that same 6 MHz.

Some broadcasters have expressed concern that if they do not do some minimal amount of High Definition video programming, they will be forced to pay for their "free" second channel. Many of the major networks are now realigning themselves and committing to a minimum High Definition video transmission schedule that may feature High Definition video in prime time and multichannel standard definition video the rest of the time.

What we do know is that at the end of the transition period, broadcasters will be forced to surrender one of their two 6MHz channels; the assumption being that they will keep their digital channel and give back the analog one. Furthermore, at end of the transition period all-digital television will be the new standard, either multichannel standard definition television or High Definition video. Advanced Television encompasses both, and ATV-compatible decoders and TV sets will be able to figure out what to display automatically.

Parting Shot

"After the first decade in widescreen high resolution video comes to a close," finishes Barry Rebo, "I'm very optimistic right now because all the market forces (broadcasters, consumers, and manufacturers) are starting to align and coordinate both their common goals and resolve their possible conflicts.

Figure 8.3—On location in Joshua Tree National Monument, CA

"There is a move in Europe to try to lock the concept of all-digital TV to the 16:9 aspect ratio. Some proponents of this idea have actually gone as far as to say that digital television sets should only be made in the 16:9 aspect ratio. To my knowledge, when American broadcasters talk about multiple channels of standard definition digital television, they're talking about multiple channels of 4:3 video, which I don't think is right. I endorse the move to make a commitment to all-digital ATV available only in 16:9."

Chapter 9

Glossary

Much of the language of High Definition video production is shared with, and taken from, traditional video and film production.

This glossary was compiled to serve as a single reference point containing explanations of words in the High Definition video context. It also, no doubt, contains more than a few familiar terms and concepts. Maybe these definitions will help make some of those clearer, too.

Terms in *italics* refer to other entries in the glossary.

ATV
The acronym for Advanced Television. In the United States, Advanced Television is the name given to the initiative to develop a digital transmission standard for HDTV and other High Definition video formats. ATV accommodates SMPTE 240M and 260M (which are HDTV production standards) but does not replace them.

Algorithm
A step-by-step description of the process by which a task is performed. A video compression algorithm describes the steps that must be performed in order to compress video signals. Examples of video compression algorithms include MPEG and motion JPEG.

Alias, Antialias

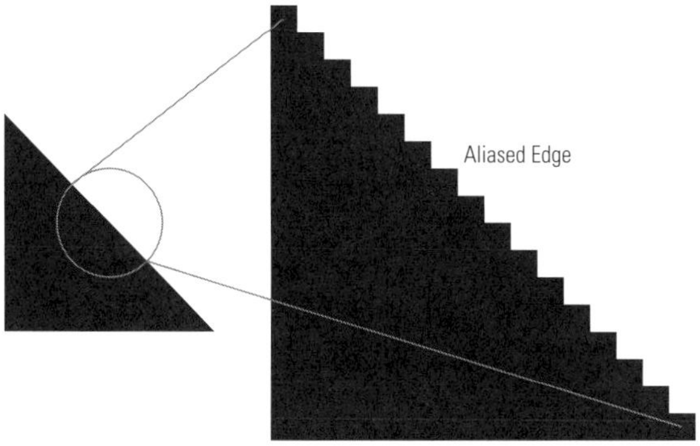

Figure 9.1—Aliased edge

Aliasing refers to false signals resulting from sampling and/or filtering errors. It is often visible as stair-stepping in high-contrast edges in raster images. Wheels that appear to spin backwards is a form of temporal aliasing. Antialiasing refers to any technique that reduces aliasing.

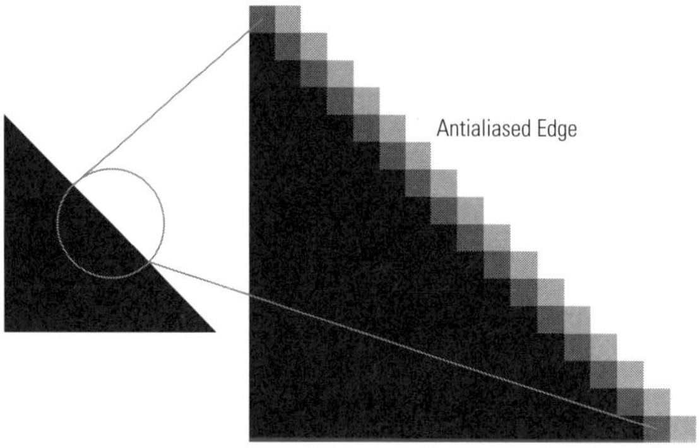

Figure 9.2—Antialiased edge

Analog
An analog signal is one that is continuously variable. If it were possible to zoom closer and closer into a waveform that represents an analog signal, the shape of the waveform would remain smooth and continuous.

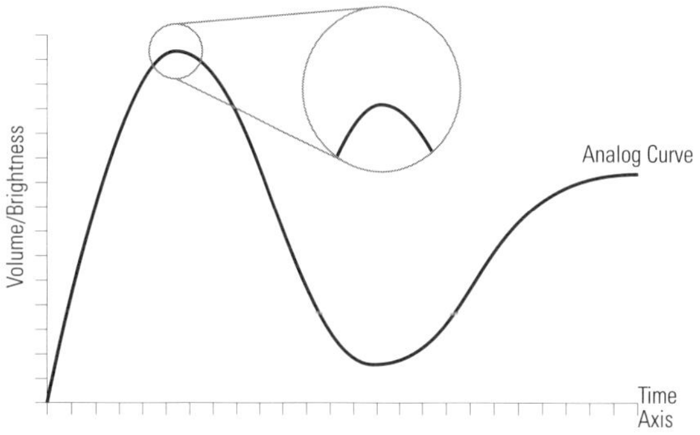

Figure 9.3—An analog curve

See also *digital, digitize.*

Antialias
See *alias.*

Bi-level Sync
See *sync.*

Bit
The smallest unit of measurement in digital systems. Bits are binary (bit comes from **bi**nary digi**t**), which means they can have either one of two values; off (0, zero), or on (1, one).

Blanking, Blanking Interval
Blanking is the nonvisible area of the video signal which generally contains sync information.

Byte
A standard unit of measurement in digital systems. A byte consists of eight bits. Using binary notation, a byte is capable of representing 256 unique values.

Bluescreen
Another word for chroma key when blue is the color used to generate the key signal.

See *chroma key*.

Chroma key
A term that refers to using color information in a video signal to generate a key signal, (also referred to as high-con, matte, and mask) for special effects and titling.

That key signal can then be used to control the combination of foreground and background images. In theory, any color can be extracted and used to generate the key signal; in practice, however, green and blue (hence green screen and bluescreen) are the most widely used colors.

Chrominance
The word used to describe the color component in television systems. It also refers to the two color difference signals in component video formats.

See *luminance*.

CIE
Commission Internationale l'Elairage, or the International Commission on Illumination. An international standards setting body whose work in the 1930s forms the theoretical and actual basis of much of the efforts to build device-independent color systems.

The CIE *color space* is a 2-dimensional model that maps the visible colors of light.

Color Space
A color space is a mathematical model describing color representation. It is called a space because the representation of the model is always 2- or 3-dimensional. The term can encompass not only the conceptual model (*CIE*, *RGB*, *YPbPr*, etc.) but also the mathematical precision of the model (8-bit RGB, etc.).

Component, Component Video
A color video image initially consists of three monochrome grayscale signals. These monochrome images represent the red, green, and blue information in the scene in front of the camera. These three monochrome signals are called components, and are referred to as *GBR* in High Definition video.

To reduce the bandwidth required to transmit and store these signals, they are compressed. Through calculation or filtering, one signal is created that contains most of the picture information in black-and-white. This is called the luminance signal. The luminance signal (which is the image displayed on a black-and-white television set) consists mostly of information from the green component of the picture because green light contains the most energy. Additional calculations or filtering is performed that results in separate, highly compressed color, or chrominance, signals.

There are several mathematical formulas used to calculate luminance and chrominance. In composite NTSC, the formula is called YIQ. In Betacam, the formula is called Y, R minus Y, B minus Y. In *HDTV*, the formula is called *YPbPr*.

When the GBR, or luminance and chrominance, components are kept separate, it is called component video. When the components are combined into a single signal, it is called *composite video*.

Composite Video

The task of the original designers of color television was to figure out how to make a color signal that could also be received on a black-and-white set. This was done by calculating, from the initial color components, a brightness signal (referred to as luminance) and separate channels of chrominance (color) information.

When the luminance image and the chrominance information are combined into a single electrical signal, the system is called composite video.

Encoding video refers to a method of combining the original components (RGB; Y, R minus Y, B minus Y, YPbPr, etc.) into one video signal. The device that does this is called an encoder.

The process of combining the luminance and chrominance channels is imperfect and causes distortion in the resulting composite video signal. It is possible, using a device called a decoder, to convert composite video back into its component signals, but the signals are never as good as the original components.

It is confusing that composite video may or may not contain sync in the same signal. When sync is incorporated into the composite video signal, it is also called composite video. When sync is not included in the composite video signal it is sometimes called noncomposite video.

Compression

A process through which the amount of information in a signal is reduced. There are many different ways to perform compression, but they basically fall into two classes, *lossless* and *lossy*.

A lossless compression method is one in which when the compressed signal or file is reconstructed (decompressed), there is absolutely no difference between the original, uncompressed signal or file, and the signal or file that has been compressed and decompressed. An example of a lossless *compression algorithm* is Huffman coding.

A lossy compression method is one in which when the compressed signal or file is decompressed, there are discernible differences, perceptible or mathematical, between the original, uncompressed signal or file, and the signal or file that has been compressed and decompressed. Examples of lossy compression algorithms include JPEG, MPEG/MPEG2, PhotoYCC, and DVI.

Compression algorithms used for still pictures take advantage of the fact that the human visual system is relatively insensitive to subtle color changes in highly detailed portions of an image (e.g., hair), but is very good at discerning small changes in broad flat expanses of color.

Compression algorithms used for motion sequences also take advantage of the fact that there are usually only very slight differences between consecutive frames. After compressing individual frames (a process called intra-frame coding), frames are compared against the frame preceding, and only the differences between current frame and the preceding frame are stored (a process called inter-frame coding). Base frames, which are compressed using intra-frame coding, and not inter-frame coding, are generated at regular intervals (usually one every second). In general, lossless algorithms support lower compression ratios than lossy algorithms.

Converting an image from GBR to YPbPr (sometimes called color space conversion) is also a form of compression. This approach takes advantage of the fact that each of the three initial R, G, and B color components contains a complete grayscale picture of the scene in front of the camera. Through calculation or filtering, redundant information is eliminated.

Compression Algorithm
The step by step description of a process (an algorithm) for reducing the size of a file or signal.

Conceal
Sometimes, errors on tape are so extensive that they cannot be corrected using the error correction algorithms in the VTR. In these cases, the VTR attempts to conceal them by attempting to recreate the value of the bad pixels by examining adjacent pixels in the immediate vicinity. Unlike corrected errors, concealed errors are never really fixed, they just get hidden. However, concealment is so good that often even a professional eye can't notice the conceals, and if it weren't for the fact that the VTR keeps track of them (the display indicates the number of conceals and their timecode locations) for you, you'd never know that they were there.

The concealment algorithms are powerful enough to compensate for the loss or damage of a head on the drum; however, in this case, the conceal is likely to be visible in most program material.

See *error correction.*

Decode, Decoding
The process of converting composite video to component video.

Digital
A digital signal is one in which the continuous analog signal has been converted into discrete steps through the process of sampling, also called digitizing. If it were possible to zoom closer and closer into a waveform that represents a digital signal, the shape of the waveform would appear to be stepped.

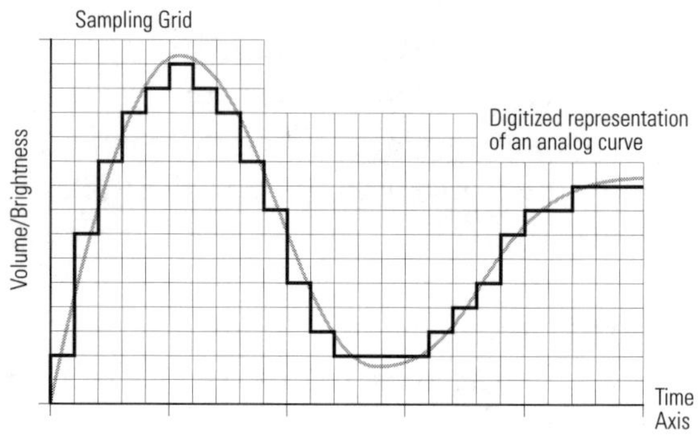

Figure 9.4—How analog curves are digitized

Digitize, Digitizing
The process of converting an analog signal to a digital one. The accuracy of the digitized representation depends on the units that comprise the sampling grid. The higher the resolution of the sampling grid, the more accurate the digitized representation of the original analog signal.

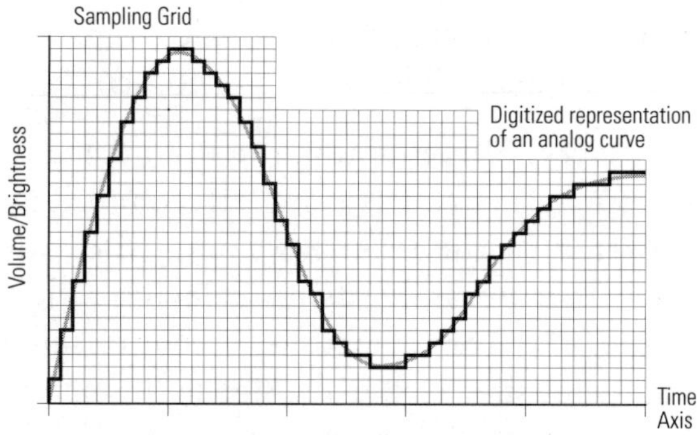

Figure 9.5—Sampling

In general, the sampling resolution of the vertical axis (volume in audio, brightness in video) is referred to in bits. Common sampling resolutions for this axis include 8-bit, or 256 levels; 10-bit, or 1024 levels; and 12-bit, or 4096 levels.

In general, the sampling resolution of the horizontal—or time—axis is referred to in kHz (thousands of cycles per second). A common sampling resolution for audio is 44.1 kHz, which is the sampling rate used for CD–ROMs.

Double system

Double system audio refers to recording picture (on film or videotape) separately from sound, usually on tape machine with timecode capability. Audio recorded on the film or videotape is usually only for reference purposes. Double system is used to distinguish between the historical process of double system film recording and single system film recording (made possible by the introduction of magnetic stripes on film); and, more recently, videotape recording.

EBR

Electron Beam Recorder. A device used to transfer electronic images to film.

ECC

Error Correction Coding.

See *error correction.*

EDL, Edit Decision List

The list of decisions made (usually) during the offline edit. EDLs are usually in computer readable form and are then used by an edit controlling system during the process of conforming, or assembling, the finished program in the online edit. Changes made to the offline EDL during the online edit can also be saved in an EDL.

Encode, Encoder, Encoding

The process of converting component video to composite video. The device used is called an encoder.

Error Correction

In any digital recording scheme, redundancy is built into the recorded data to make it possible to reconstruct data in the case of partial tape failure. High Definition digital VTRs are no exception to this rule, and because of the huge amounts of data involved, error correction coding (or ECC) is especially important.

One advantage of the way ECC is implemented in digital VTRs is that when a tape is digitally dubbed, bad or missing pixels are fixed.

GBR

Green, Blue, Red; the preferred description of RGB in High Definition video. It is important to pay attention to this because it easy to think RGB and hook up cables incorrectly.

HD-MAC

High Definition-Multiplexed Analog Component. An analog transmission format.

HDTV

High Definition Television. Alternatively:

> Hard Duty Television, Heavy Duty Television, High Density Television, High Destiny Television, Highly Difficult Television, High Dollar Television, Highly Deluded Television, Highly Doubtful Television, Hot Damn Television, Hot Dog Television, Howdy Doody Television, Hunky Dory Television

Header Descriptor Block

The ATV digital transmission standard is designed to be extensible, which means that the six formats supported in the original standard can be added to as technology improves. In the ATV system change is accommodated through the use of a header descriptor block. Key parameters of the video signal, such as number of scan lines and number of frames or fields per second, are encoded digitally in the header descriptor block.

The ATV receiver/decoder reads the header descriptor block and configures itself to decode and display the incoming video signal properly.

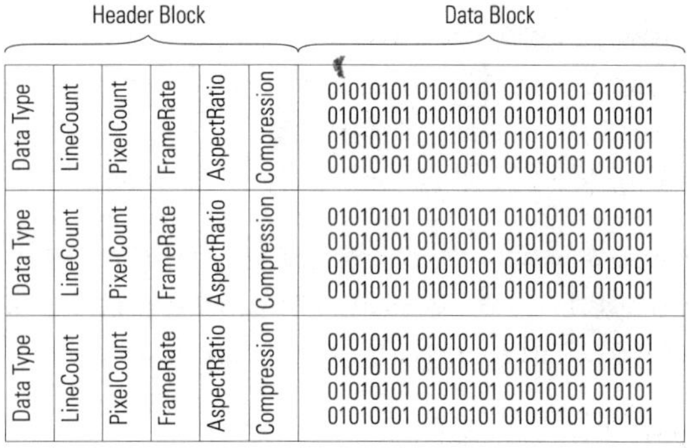

Figure 9.6—ATV header descriptor block schematic

Each of the blocks in the header descriptor contains a specific piece of information that the ATV decoder reads and interprets. These types of information include, but are not limited to:

1 Data type (still, motion, audio [number of channels])

2 Type of compression algorithm(s) used

3 Color model

4 Frame/field rate

5 Number of lines

6 Number of pixels/line

7 Aspect ratio

The header descriptor definition has been designed so that as equipment capabilities increase, ATV can evolve to meet these changes more easily.

Interlace, Interlaced

A moving NTSC video image is composed of a sequence of still images called frames, and each frame is composed of two sequential fields, one containing the odd numbered lines, the other containing the even numbered lines. The method of combining the two fields into one frame is called interlacing.

The smoothness of motion in an image is determined by the number of still pictures presented each second. For example, film presents 24 images (frames) per second; NTSC, 59.94 images (fields) per second; PAL, 50 images (fields) per second; and SMPTE 240M HDTV 60 images (fields) per second.

See *noninterlaced.*

JPEG

JPEG stands for Joint Photographic Expert Group, and is a type of compression algorithm used to reduce the amount of data in still pictures and motion sequences.

Lossless

A term used to categorize a type of compression algorithm.

A lossless compression algorithm is one in which when the compressed signal or file is reconstructed (decompressed), there is absolutely no difference between the original, uncompressed signal or file, and the signal or file that has been compressed and decompressed. Examples of lossless compression algorithms include Huffman coding and run-length encoding, or RLE.

Lossy

A term used to categorize a type of compression algorithm.

A lossy compression algorithm is one in which when the compressed signal or file is decompressed, there are discernible differences, perceptible or mathematical, between the original, uncompressed signal or file, and the signal or file that has been compressed and decompressed. Examples of lossy compression algorithms include *JPEG, MPEG*/MPEG2, PhotoYCC, and DVI.

Luminance
Luminance refers to the brightness component of a video signal. It is composed primarily of the information from the green component of the video image.

Matte
A matte is an image that is used to combine (or composite) two or more images or video signals together into a single image or video signal. Color or values of gray in the matte image can be used to represent different levels of transparency ranging from fully opaque to fully transparent.

MPEG
MPEG stands for Motion Picture Expert Group, and is a type of compression algorithm used to reduce the amount of data in motion sequences.

Motion Control
The use of a computerized and motorized platform to be able to control camera movements very precisely and repeatably for animation and special effects purposes.

MUSE
Abbreviation for multiple sub-Nyquist encoding. MUSE is a compression scheme used, almost exclusively in Japan, for broadcasting HDTV programming.

See *Nyquist.*

Noninterlaced
A video display format which draws each image frame in its entirety, sequentially, line by line, before beginning to draw the next frame. Noninterlaced displays require twice the system bandwidth of interlaced displays to display the same resolution image. Noninterlaced displays can have less flicker than interlaced displays, and are particularly good at displaying still images with fine details, such as small typographic features.

See *progressive.*

Nyquist
A mathematician who determined the fundamental minimal sampling frequency, called the Nyquist limit, required to accurately digitize an analog signal.

In order to represent an analog signal accurately digitally, it is necessary to sample at least twice the highest frequency that needs to be represented accurately. Thus, the 44.1 kHz sampling frequency of audio CDs is theoretically capable of accurately reproducing sounds up to 22.05 kHz.

One Inch, 1"
A video format that refers to a specific tape format (one-inch open reel) and its associated player/recorder, as in "...a one-inch VTR." 1" digital HD VTRs were produced in both analog and digital formats. The older analog 1" VTRs (which are generally considered to be obsolete) support only the older 5:3 image aspect ratio and bi-level sync.

Overscan
In NTSC, the displayed image is smaller than the actual image. The parts of the image that cannot be seen are called overscan. Overscan, which was originally introduced to account for manufacturing tolerances, gave rise to the concepts safe title area and safe action area. As newer television sets with digital circuitry are designed, the reasons for, and amount of overscan is diminished.

Pixel
Contraction of picture element. In digital systems, images are created, stored, and displayed in grids. Each square of the grid is a pixel.

Progressive, Progressive Scan
Another term for noninterlaced. A progressively scanned image is one in which each line of the picture is drawn sequentially with all lines being drawn in each frame.

Resolution
Resolution is a measure of the ability of a system to resolve detail. Higher resolution systems are able to resolve more detail than lower resolution systems.

In television systems, resolution is measured by pointing a camera at a specially designed test chart. This test chart consists mainly of black lines drawn in patterns where the lines get progressively closer and closer together. Each pair of black lines is separated by a white space. If it is possible to see the white spaces between the lines, then the camera and monitor combination (and, if the image is recorded, the VTR as well), can be said to resolve that many TV lines (TVL, not to be confused with scan lines).

The ability of a television system to resolve detail is based on a lot of factors, including the quality of the lens, the size of the scanning target, the size of the electron beam scanning the target or the size of the individual pixels on the CCD chip, and whether or not the image or signal is compressed or encoded, among other factors.

RGB
A color space. RGB stands for Red, Green, Blue. RGB is the preferred name for this color space for computer graphics and print. In High Definition video, it is properly referred to as GBR.

See *GBR*.

SFX
Acronym for special effects.

SMPTE
Acronym for the Society of Motion Picture and Television Engineers.

Safe Action Area
An area within the picture frame within which all important action is framed so that it is visible within the areas of the image likely to be unaffected by transient video effects.

Sample, Sampling
A sample is a single digitized value. Sampling is part of the process of converting an analog signal to a digital one.

When referring to the quality of a sampled signal, two variables are discussed; the number of samples per second (the sampling frequency), and the quantization (the number of discrete values that can be differentiated).

Sampling frequency is measured in kHz, or thousands of samples per second. Typical sampling frequencies for digital audio are 11, 22, 33, 44.1, and 48 KHz. CD-quality audio is sampled at 44.1 kHz. The sampling frequency determines the highest-pitched sound that can be accurately reproduced.

It is a general rule (called the Nyquist limit) that the sampling frequency must be twice the highest frequency to be accurately reproduced. Thus, the 44.1 kHz audio CD is theoretically capable of accurately reproducing audio waveforms up to 22.05 kHz.

The quantization of the sample is measured in bits. The typical quantization for digital audio is 16 bits, or 65,536 discrete values. 20-bit sampling is common for professional applications.

Video sampling is referred to in terms of multiples of subcarrier frequency as well as bit depth. A typical sampling frequency for video is 4:2:2, which means that the Y (luminance) component of the image is sampled at 4X the subcarrier frequency, and both color difference components are recorded at 2X the subcarrier frequency. Quantization is typically 8 bits (256 levels), but 10 bit sampling (1024 levels) formats are becoming more and more common.

The sampling rate for SMPTE 240M and SMPTE 260M is approximately 75 MHz. 260M supports both 8- and 10-bit quantization.

Speed

High Definition VTRs require preroll time before the tape is up to speed and locked. The film term "speed" is used to indicate that a VTR is rolling and ready to record.

Standard Definition Video

NTSC, PAL, and SECAM.

Sync

There are a number of components in video systems: cameras, VTRs, monitors, switchers, effects devices, etc. In order for all these devices to display the same image in the same timing relationship, it is necessary to synchronize them by providing them with information about when in the electrical signal each new field and line starts. This is done by providing sync pulses with the video signals. There are two types of sync pulses, horizontal and vertical.

In some cases, the sync information is a part of the video signal, at other times, sync is carried on a separate wire. The video part of the signal describes the visual image; the sync part of the signal is not visible.

Video signals can be transmitted without sync information combined with the video. This is called noncomposite video. When sync information is added, this is called composite video.

Sync is used to describe where fields and lines start and end. In order to combine different video sources, the fields and lines from each source need to start and end at the same time relative to each other. The process of synchronizing the start and end times of two or more video sources is called genlocking.

Sync pulses in NTSC are referred to as bi-level because they are composed of two voltage levels. HDTV equipment uses tri-level sync.

The diagram below presents a schematic representation of the HDTV tri-level sync signal, with key timing information. For complete signal timing information, refer to the SMPTE 240M and 260M specifications.

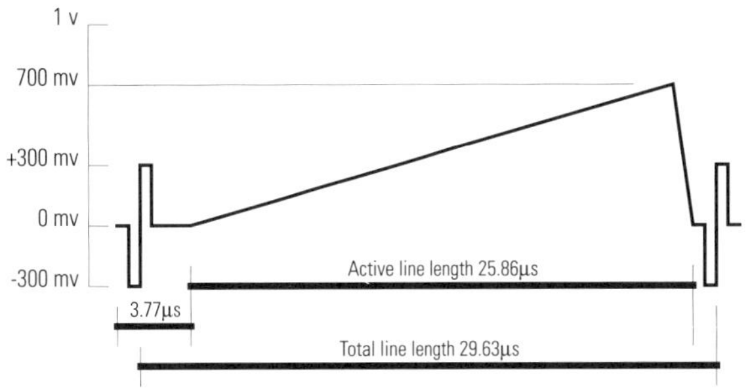

Figure 9.7—The shape of tri-level sync

Telecine

A device used to transfer film images to video.

Transcode, Transcoding

The process of converting one form of component video to another form, for example, RGB to Y, R-Y, B-Y.

The process of converting component video to composite video is called encoding. The process of converting composite video to component video is called decoding.

Tri-level sync

See *sync*.

Ultimatte

A high quality blue/green screen (or chroma key) video compositing device. Ultimatte is sometimes also used generically to describe chroma key compositing.

UNIHI or 1/2"

A specific High Definition video tape format (half-inch cassette) and its associated player/recorder, as in "...a UNIHI VTR." The video signal recorded in the UNIHI format is analog YPbPr and is not full SMPTE 240M-spec bandwidth.

YPbPr

A color space model and mathematical transform for compressing image and video data. Y refers to the luminance or brightness component of the image. Pb and Pr refer to the color difference components.

Index

A

B

C

D

E

F

G

H

I

J

K

L

R

S